# Tesla's Words

*A Stunning Utopia of the Future*

# Tesla's Words

*A Stunning Utopia of the Future*

## Written by Ellis Oswalt
with
*Art by Jina Park*

# ACKNOWLEDGMENTS

This drama is adapted from *My Inventions*, the autobiography of Nikola Tesla. A special thanks to my friend Doug Pecot, whose engineering knowledge and consistent help was invaluable for telling this story. Carol Chester helped keep this book compelling by helping me deliberate over ever single comma. I am additionally very thankful for the scientific consultation of David Chester, PhD in physics.

A gigantic thanks must also be given to Nick Lonchar and the Tesla Science Foundation for helping to promote this little paperback to a wider audience. I am extremely grateful that after the initial release of this book, I was interviewed about Nikola Tesla by the *Australian Associated Press* as well as Serbian national public broadcasting *PTC*.

Dedicated to Nikola Tesla
July 10, 1856 – Jan. 7, 1943

# Table of Contents

# INTRODUCTION

In his prime, Nikola Tesla was one of the most famous people alive. In stark contrast, only a few years after his death, he was completely forgotten for decades to follow. His name was absent from the history books used in American classrooms and to this day, most people continue to use his inventions on an hourly basis without knowing his name.

Tesla came to New York City from Europe and transformed the ways in which the entire world uses electricity. Despite his importance, most people today are still unsure of what, exactly, Nikola Tesla actually contributed to technology. Most people associate his name with the electric car company made famous by Elon Musk. The auto company was named after Nikola Tesla because their cars are powered by Tesla's induction motor, but Tesla himself never ventured into the automobile business.

Tesla invented the first wireless remote control devices, radio, and the earliest usable forms of neon and fluorescent lighting[1]. The unit for measuring the strength of a magnet or magnetic field is even called a "Tesla." You might also call Tesla the "Grandfather of Robotics." He built a large toy boat out of steel that he could control with a remote. It was the first of its kind when he showed it to the world in 1898 at Madison Square Garden. Within a period of just a few short years, the techniques he produced made electricity not only

---

[1] On neon and fluorescent light:

Tesla invented a similar style of lighting almost a decade before Peter Cooper Hewitt patented the mercury vapor lamp widely considered to be the first successful fluorescent light. Tesla's invention was not the same as a modern fluorescent light, but Tesla's "phosphorescent light" was the first usable lightbulb that operated without using a filament, like Edison's famous incandescent lightbulb. It was a precursor to modern fluorescent light.

Scholars dispute whether it was at the Chicago World's Fair of 1893 or in 1899, but Tesla displayed ornate lighting in long, skinny tubes that had been bent into artful shapes and spelled words. Once lit, these lights glowed in a rainbow of colors and existing photos show their resemblance to modern neon lights. Tesla's display was years before neon lighting was patented in 1915 by Georges Claude. Tesla's early neon lights may or may not have been the same as Claude's, but it is clear that Tesla beat him to the punch for building the first working concept.

safer, but affordable and accessible to the masses.

Tesla's system of alternating current made electrical use possible on a large scale, but he still wanted to go much bigger with his ideas on how to distribute electricity. At the height of his popularity, Tesla's wireless lightbulbs were a well-known achievement. Tesla first publicly demonstrated his lightbulbs at the Chicago World Fair in 1893. It was an advanced technology that continues to remain unavailable to most of us today, one hundred years later.

All our wireless products eventually need to return home to a wired connection in order to be recharged. In addition, these products rely on batteries that wreak havoc on the environment once replaced and disposed. Tesla's technology for wireless power meant that electricity would flow from a transmitter and float invisibly through the air, flowing straight into a device to provide power.

Imagine your television, toaster, microwave, floor lamp, and stereo all turned on and working without ever having to plug them into a wall outlet, and without ever charging a battery. Imagine never having to charge your cellphone. This was Nikola Tesla's vision.

Tesla used wireless lightbulbs to show the world his larger idea of building a society free from wires. The bulbs only produced a small fraction of heat compared to traditional bulbs, and they could be held in-hand when lit, which Tesla loved to use for dramatic purposes. The wireless electrical energy used to power the bulbs was sent through the air directly into the bulb.

Tesla gave private lectures about this technology at Columbia University and the Royal Institute of Great Britain, among many other institutions across the United States and Europe. This world tour of lectures about his wireless technologies is one of the most important yet forgotten details about the story of Nikola Tesla and his legacy. Using a lightbulb was a simple and effective visual aid to show the world the possibilities this new technology could offer. In today's terms, Tesla offered a way of creating Wi-Fi—but instead of internet access, a single router would supply wireless electrical power to every appliance in your home.

There would be no need to plug your toaster into the wall; Tesla's proposed device would collect energy from a nearby power station and send it wirelessly to your electrical appliances at home. Again, imagine never having to charge your cellphone. Imagine having an electric car that is always charging from a nearby radius. By touring the world with his wireless lightbulbs, Tesla showed us that this could all become the reality of the future.

If all of this is true, how is it possible that this man's story was so easily forgotten? Maybe some of this can be explained by sheer bad timing. Just months after his death, the U.S. Supreme Court in 1943 finally ruled in a long-standing court battle that Nikola Tesla, *not* Guglielmo Marconi, should be credited as the inventor of radio. Marconi had filed the first radio patent and years later won the 1909 Nobel Prize in physics for it, a Nobel Prize this evidence suggests may rightfully belong to Tesla.

The long-standing disputes regarding what Nikola Tesla actually did and did not invent only adds mystery and myth to his story. Legitimate historians, biographers, and other reporters from reputable institutions find themselves with confusing and contradicting information about the man. The past isn't always easy to decipher, and it is as if Nikola

Tesla fell through the cracks of history. The story of his life takes one bizarre turn after another and it's no wonder why so many reporters have chosen to leave out controversial parts of his story.

In his autobiography, Tesla describes his final project, which he never finished due to financial constraints. As early as 1891, Nikola Tesla was dreaming up ideas of building the world's first internet; it was his last great project. Using the technology from his wireless lightbulb, he described a worldwide system that could be built to transfer photographs, letters, voice, music, and more, to and from any point around the globe in an instant. It would have also functioned as an early form of GPS-like navigation system and, furthermore, it would have replaced the existing electrical power infrastructure with a completely wireless one. In other words, no power lines would be needed, and every home would receive electrical power wirelessly at a low cost sent from large antennae. His dream was to give free power to every home.

During the six years that followed his performance at the Chicago World's Fair, Tesla was busy building his enterprises in partnership with George Westinghouse. Tesla eagerly waited for his chance to return to the idea of wireless power, but other commitments kept his hands busy. Not only was he managing his first business, his fame had launched him into a social life amongst high society. Tesla was thrilled to live among the elite. But in 1899, he fled his ballroom lifestyle in New York to set up a laboratory in Colorado Springs, where he could seclude himself in experimentation without distractions and with much more space. Tesla stayed in Colorado for a year, keeping a detailed journal of his daily experiments and their results.

Tesla then returned to New York and gathered the necessary funding from his close financial backer and friend, J.P. Morgan. He began to build the world's first wireless power transmission station on Long Island. Tesla was building a station with the promise to Morgan that it would enable private wireless communication across the Atlantic Ocean. However, when Tesla revealed to Morgan the station would also provide abundant wireless electrical energy to the surrounding area at no cost to consumers, Morgan pulled his funding from the project.

Morgan and Tesla had been close friends. Morgan would often reserve a seat for Tesla at the table with his family on Thanksgiving Day. As close as they were, Morgan never wasted a moment of his attention on Tesla again after the tower at Wardenclyffe on Long Island, New York. He was offended Tesla would do something so counterintuitive with the money he had invested, and Tesla in turn was furious that Morgan had no interest in making the world a better place simply because it affected his bank account. The matter ended their friendship.

Morgan was the only person in the United States wealthy enough to fund the venture, and Tesla never recovered once Morgan pulled his funding. Tesla spent the following decades of his life in financial struggle, having thrown all of his poker chips into one pot, and having lost. It wasn't Tesla's first large financial mis-step, but it was his last. He spent the rest of his life living on credit while staying in a room at the Hotel New Yorker, paid for by the Westinghouse Corporation. Once Tesla lost the confidence of J.P. Morgan, he spent the next few decades trying to pursue the only other entity that could afford to fund the project—the United States military.

Tesla never secured any contracts with the Department of Defense, but as soon as he died of natural causes at the age of 87 in 1943, the FBI raided his hotel room in fear that any ideas he had been offering to sell to the U.S. military could fall into enemy hands. Tesla had spoken in newspaper interviews about a particle beam weapon that could vaporize solid material and about missiles that could be fired from across the planet to a faraway country. At the time of Tesla's death, the U.S. was heavily involved with World War II. Dr. John Trump, the uncle of the 45th President of the United States, was the engineer tasked with analyzing all of the documents found in the hotel room seizure. Dr. John Trump made a public statement days later saying that nothing of use was found among the papers and personal belongings of Nikola Tesla.

Although interest in Tesla's life has resurfaced in the last few decades, his actual writings have largely gone unnoticed. The six chapters that make up his autobiography were originally published in *Electrical Experimenter Magazine* as part of an ongoing series. Now these writings are in the public domain. You can find well-preserved copies of these magazine editions online, just look for Tesla's face on the cover as you search the online archives of *Electrical Experimenter*.

Tesla's autobiography is a dusty old book that still holds a lot of relevance. It is infinitely strange to hear Tesla personally tell you the story of his life. Pretty quickly, he gets comfortable enough to confess living a life filled with regular hallucinations. As he tells us about his personal life, the story builds into a seemingly science-fiction vision of the future that involves self-driving vehicles and infinite amounts of energy to power them wirelessly.

For the same reasons that almost no one will read a work of Shakespeare at leisure, most people would not enjoy reading Nikola Tesla's autobiography. It is literature from the past that cannot be understood at a glance. It's not something modern people read for enjoyment, but rather a classical work that requires study in order to understand the language and context.

This edition is a simplified version for a 21st century audience. Tesla will speak to you personally and share all the details of his rise and fall. Some of Tesla's story will always remain a mystery, and I make no attempts to produce answers to those mysteries. I fill in some small gaps with a heavy amount of research and a tiny bit of artistic license, but you are essentially reading everything Tesla wanted his audience to know.

Finally, one last note. Tesla was well educated in engineering and world literature. He could read and speak eight languages. He alluded to obscure biblical figures, ancient Greek philosophers and other classic allegories every chance he could get in his writings, most of which I have omitted for simplicity. While most of his writing may seem dull for a 21st century audience, there are genuine flares of poetry scattered throughout his writing. I've included some of Nikola Tesla's most interesting written and spoken words **IN BOLD** throughout the chapters, easily identifiable to the reader as Tesla's actual quotes. These are *Tesla's Words*.

*"Why Shouldn't truth be stranger than fiction? Fiction after all, has to make sense."*

—Mark Twain

# Tesla's Words

*A Stunning Utopia of the Future*

# PART ONE

It has been my supreme pleasure to live life as an inventor of the highest status. The inventor's purpose is to accelerate society evermore towards the idea of utopia. I am honored and blessed to have lived this life and to be categorized as one of the most successful inventors to date, amongst a very short list. I have done my part, and when I leave this beautiful Earth, I will have already left humankind in a much better condition than when I entered into this world. My life has been a magnificent journey of the type that almost none have had the privilege to experience. I have watched my own ideas become reality on such a grand scale that they have transformed societies across the globe and they will continue to do so when I am gone.

I suppose it is necessary to start at the beginning, isn't it? Well, I was born in the small village of Smiljan[2] to wonderful parents in a

---

[2] In modern day Croatia.

beautiful country home. We had horses, arable land, and a handful of hired servants. I have fond memories of the fresh air, flocks of geese, and other sights and senses of the countryside. Growing up in such a place was truly the best way imaginable to nurture my creative young mind. I have always felt gratitude for my homeland.

At a very early age, I became awfully shy. One contributing factor to this pattern of behavior began when I witnessed my older brother's violent death from being pummeled by one of our horses. The horse was startled by the thunder and lightning of a sudden storm. I still remember the loud crack my brother's breaking bones produced, and some nights still, I recall what I saw that night as my arm hairs stiffen upwards. In my memory, the snap of his breaking bones still rings as loud as the thunder that startled the horse.

My brother's death shattered my parents and I imagine it was the reasoning behind their continual gloom for many years after his death. This may also be the reason I developed a shyness. I always struggled to cheer them up. I tried and tried for months and years. There was nothing I could do to lift their sadness. During that time, whenever I did anything worth noting, they would continue to be sad. I think seeing my vivacious childhood made them feel their loss even more. The impact of my brother's death on our family stunted my self-confidence during those critical years of early development.

I very much do not want to talk about my family because family is so deeply personal and private. But when I was asked to write the story of my life as a series, I started to consider that I must reveal these intimate details of my life. They are necessary to give a true account. So next, I will start with my mother, whom I miss dearly.

She was an astounding and brilliant woman. My mother came from a long line of inventors on her father's side and would have easily become a successful inventor herself had she decided to remove herself from the small town life. Out of both of my parents, it was she who passed down to me the blood of an inventor. Her father and grandfather had made many commonplace improvements to daily life and agriculture with their inventions. She was highly creative and a true workhorse who followed in their footsteps. With her bare hands, she made all sorts of tools and little gadgets to help with her labors. She was constantly building and crafting.

She designed beautiful garments from cloth she herself wove and spun. If that wasn't impressive enough, she made the clothes all the way from planting the seeds in the soil, harvesting the plants, and then plucking the fibers before she would spin them into wearable, dashing clothes. She even hand-built the looms and other tools used in making the clothes. Her clothing was the envy of all the other women in the village. She made clothes for everyone in the family, including my four other siblings. She even made most of the furniture. She worked endlessly from sunrise to late into the night. She was a true force of nature and a prolific nurturer until the end. **When she was past sixty, her fingers were still nimble enough to tie three knots in an eyelash.** I have been so lucky to have her and I could not have had a more amazing mother.

My father was a priest of the Serbian Orthodox Church, and since my birth, he intended for me to be a clergyman to follow in his footsteps. This put me under a considerable amount of stress because I desperately wanted to be an engineer from a young age. The dream seemed so impossible. If I were ever to even bring up the subject with my father, he would erupt into a fit. I never at that time imagined I could actually become an engineer when I grew up. It was practically forbidden.

Although my father was a priest, he had received a military education before choosing the path of teaching the Holy Bible and performing sermons every week. His father had also been a military man who served with the rank of officer in Napoleon's grand army. You can imagine the rigid nature of his personality. He was a highly intelligent man as well. His mind was always searching for answers to the difficult questions of philosophy.

My father was a poet and writer as well. He had a robust memory and would regularly burst into reciting literary works in many languages. His face would form a sly grin as he would often say to us that if the classics were lost, he could rewrite some of them from memory, word for word. He was a truly well-beloved and well-known preacher for many miles, adored for his powerful sermons.

He was as stern a father as they come, but he did have a soft side full of intelligent humor. Once, I was with my father as he was taking a friend on a carriage ride. The friend had unknowingly allowed his expensive fur coat to come into full contact with the muddy carriage wheel. As my father witnessed this he said to him flatly, **"Pull in your coat; you are ruining my tire."**

To give you another example of his humor, I remember my father once said a funny quip to one of our hired servants. This particular servant, Mane, suffered from cross-eyed vision and was employed for outdoor labors. One day as Mane was chopping wood, my father became startled at the reckless chopping as he stood nearby. He said, **"For God's sake, Mane, do not strike at what you are looking but at what you intend to hit."** It was commonplace to find my father talking to himself or even passionately arguing with himself. He would speak in several different funny voices to represent the opposing arguers as he debated his own thoughts. He was just as stern as he was gentle and he was just as smart as he was odd.

Although I fully credit my mother for handing down any hereditary inventive prowess I obtained, my father played a large role in my development. He gave me many daily exercises in my early life to train my mind, and they surely had an impact on my growing brain. He would have me repeat long sentences, perform mental calculations, and would even sit down with me as we carefully looked into one another's faces, guessing each other's thoughts as an exercise in empathy and perception.

Perhaps the primary reason for my early shyness, and a much more significant one, was due to a strange and frequent health condition, for lack of a better term, of body and mind. I would see things: ultra-vivid and lifelike hallucinations. Floating images and great bursts of flashing light would strike me without notice at all hours of the day. **In some instances I have seen all the air around me filled with tongues of living flame.** I can remember my teeth chattering uncontrollably out of fear many times as a child.

The condition was very hard to handle in those early years of my life. When I was being spoken to and an object was mentioned by name, just hearing the words would very often trigger my brain into hallucinating the objects mentioned in the conversation. The hallucinations seemed to always be connected to whatever thoughts were floating through my mind. So, if my father asked me to fetch his boots, it would turn out to be a more difficult task than he knew.

I would look towards the coat rack, see a pair of boots, then reach my hand outwards towards the boots only to find myself empty handed as I reached for boots that did not exist. I was unable to distinguish which objects I saw were real and which ones my brain had created. It made parts of my childhood very troubling. I practically had no one with whom I could confide about this, and it made the pain of losing my brother so much more unbearable because I was told he may have had similar issues. It would have been a relief to share that confusion with someone who could understand.

I still have the hallucinations, although the attacks were by far the worst during my childhood and early adulthood. I have never met an expert in psychology or biology who could come up with a sound answer as to why they occur. According to their responses, it would seem that I am the only person on God's Earth to have ever suffered these peculiar experiences. I don't know how that could be true.

I realize this all sounds like nonsense. Please believe me, these hallucinations are not to be associated with what you might call a psychotic disorder, such as schizophrenia. I have always been in possession of a sound and healthy mind, free of delusions. My mental faculties have never failed me and these have never been the type of hallucinations that come with extreme mental illnesses. I assure you, I am well.

At first, and for a long time, the hallucinations were only of things I had actually seen in real life. The hallucinations would very often be associated with something I had a strong emotional response towards, or whatever I happened to be thinking about at that specific time. For example, once I had attended a funeral with my parents. It was probably my first funeral, making it a new experience for me. I was more alert and aware of my surroundings, just as any person tends to be when having a new experience. The stimulation was a perfect recipe to trigger my hallucinatory responses.

I was surrounded by people mourning and chatting at the funeral; there were speeches and a sermon. The sight of the old dead man's face lying there in his open casket left only a small impression at the time. Later than night, however, I was thinking deeply upon the ideas of death and mortality for the first time as a child. As my thoughts tended to materialize into a hallucination, I was given a much deeper impression of his face yet again that very evening. I was truly terrified as I continued to see his lifeless face wherever I looked upon the walls and ceiling.

When the images scared me, my only defense was to try to think of something else. If my mind could just let go and think of other things and objects, I would hallucinate about those things instead. This is much easier said than done, however. Believe it or not, once an idea took hold of my mind, it was very hard not to think about it. It took me years to master this simple act.

One day, I was having trouble doing just this. An image that bothered me was appearing everywhere I looked. I simply couldn't focus my mind to think of something happy that could replace my uncomfortable hallucination, so I walked outside. Maybe a walk would help calm me, I thought. After all, a walk would change my view and my immediate visual field.

Going for sudden walks to change my mood was a great turning point for me. I slowly gained control over these hallucinations. Soon, I found if I was not anxious and I approached my hallucinations with calmness and a positive outlook, it became very fun for me. Oh, what a time! When I began to do this, I no longer hallucinated only the things I had seen before—I began to hallucinate things I had never seen. When I learned to just let go and enjoy my thoughts, I was taken for quite a ride.

My only explanation is that somehow the part of the brain which creates vivid, never-before-seen images while dreaming was somehow connected to my waking brain. It is truly fascinating to me and I believe that in years to come, scientists will make striking discoveries about the complexity of the human brain. Perhaps one day there will be a machine that can connect to the human brain that will show projections of our working thoughts in the form of moving pictures.

I went on countless journeys experiencing dream-like travels simply by staring out into space. As a restless teenager, I would sit in a chair and just take a few breaths. I would look upon the wall for many minutes until the smooth surface would begin to form gentle waves. As I continued to gaze, eventually the wall would cave in completely and then morph into another world. I met people inside these "awake-dreams." I went to places, cities, and countries I had never known before. These were not real places, of course, but as real to me as the typewriter I see before me now. I had conversations and overheard stories and experienced an entire world separate from our reality.

Because it was so fun, I did this constantly until I was about seventeen. Right around that age, I began to realize these images I saw were truly a gift from God. This was because I was becoming passionate about inventing for the first time. So, to my inexpressible joy, I had harnessed my abilities and could control the hallucinations by that point. *I could see what I wanted to see.*

For my inventions, I did not need to produce models or draft drawings, and many times, I did not even need to conduct experiments. I could imagine all the tiniest details of my inventions and literally see a manifestation right in front of my eyes as I looked out into space. I could imagine the inventions and they would appear before me in midair. I could lift my arm and outstretch it, watching my hand pass right through the object I was hallucinating. I was born to be an inventor.

*"Then, inevitably, in the stillness of night, a vivid picture of the scene would thrust itself before my eyes and persist despite all my efforts to banish it. Sometimes it would even remain fixed in space though I pushed my hand through it."*

—Nikola Tesla

# PART TWO

Now that you know the specific strangeness of my life, I can be completely honest with you. I am positive that I would have lived a life dedicated to science even without my divine blessings, but to what extent, I do not know. It is an understatement to say that I approach the creation of new ideas and concepts far differently than any other inventor. My power of visualization is a tool that makes my inventive work fly by all the more quickly.

You can't imagine how frustrating it is for me to sit by and watch other people work to design a machine the typical way. If I had to waste all my energy into papers, schematics, drawings, drafts, scale models, and the like, I would probably need to walk out of the boardroom and let out a scream several times a day. Gladly, I do not have to put up with any of that. My way of creating machines and inventions is, simply put, more highly evolved.

There is no need for me to quickly spring into action in my work. When I find an idea, I simply let that idea grow within my imagination. I stare ahead into space, and before my eyes, I watch my idea play out, making changes and improvements as I please. It is almost like watching from a film projector. I can take any invention in progress and rearrange the structure, or flip it around completely to examine the backside. I do this all without exerting myself, or dealing with actual tools and machines.

**It is absolutely immaterial to me whether I run my turbine in thought or test it in my shop. I even note if it is out of balance. There is no difference whatever; the results are the same. In this way, I am able to rapidly develop and perfect a conception without touching anything.** I work this way until I can see no more room possible for improvement, and then I begin construction. **Invariably, my device works as I conceived that it should, and the experiment comes out exactly as I planned it.** I am now 63 years of age. In the past 20 years, I have not made a single mistake creating new inventions with this method.

The possibilities are limitless. **There is scarcely a subject that cannot be examined beforehand, from the available theoretical and practical data.** We have our physics, calculus, and geometry. An infinite number of inventions are waiting to be created with these existing tools. If you take these tools and spend time with them, a truer view of the natural world will come into focus.

My hallucinations as a child were scary, but these days it does not bother me one bit to see a hallucination. However, that early trauma from my gifts helped me develop a strong sense of reality that I have difficulty expressing to other people, at least with little success. **The incessant mental exertion developed my powers of observation and enabled me to discover a truth of great importance.**

I am referring to the automatic nature of the brain. Eventually, it dawned on me that all the hallucinations I suffered in those early years followed my seeing of actual things. I would remember significant moments, and it was an automatic response for my mind to return to those images again throughout my life.

I think this happens with all people, except I hallucinate the memories that grab my attention throughout the day. The point being, this is an automatic response. We are triggered to think certain thoughts when we have certain physical experiences, like memories returning to us from a smell or a taste. It is automatic and unstoppable.

When I realized the automatic nature of our brains, it changed the way I managed my hallucinations. When I was young and under a dark hallucinatory spell of seeing things that terrified me, it prompted me to take some time to think about where and when I had originally seen the objects in real life beforehand, and simply trace my memory for the events and conditions that sprung me into a terrible thought-trap. I would consider the social conditions, my own emotional state, and any other psychological factors. **After a while, this effort grew to be almost automatic, and I gained great facility in connecting cause and effect.**

Free will as a concept slowly revealed itself to be an illusion. I realized that all of my thoughts, all of my hopes, all of my cravings were not truly my own. **Soon I became aware, to my surprise, that every thought I conceived was suggested by an external impression.** The rich colors and smells, as well as everything else that acts upon the senses in the world outside of our brains, are all stimuli that drive our choices for us. As far as I can tell, chemical reactions can sometimes govern my decisions more than I myself do.

We do not choose a favorite food or favorite color. We do not choose to like or dislike something. These things choose us and we have no control over their power to possess us. We cannot access the part of our subconscious mind that is drawn to make these choices for us. Though, perhaps there is free will in the ability to recognize our own behavioral patterns and work slowly to change them.

**In the course of time, it became perfectly evident to me that I was merely an automation endowed with power of movement responding to the stimuli of the sense organs and thinking and acting accordingly.** We are machines, and much of our behavior can be described as robotic programming.

**The practical result of this was the art of telautomatics which has been so far carried out only in an imperfect manner.** In the future, there will be no need for human workers to perform hard labors. **I believe that mechanisms can be produced which will act as if**

**possessed of reason, to a limited degree, and will create a revolution in many commercial and industrial departments.** Because of my inventions, machines will be able to follow our commands, and life will be unrecognizable from the way we currently live.

I formulated these ideas throughout my life as a direct result of the many hallucinations I experienced. All my life long I have had haunting visions and strange gifts and flashing lights that seize my body in a spell of hallucination.

I was about twelve years old the first time I was able to eject an uncomfortable hallucination from my sight through sheer willpower. However, I have never had an ounce of control over seeing the erratic flashes of light of which I have also mentioned. These were possibly my most confusing episodes and they usually happened when I was very excited or found myself in danger.

The strength of these episodes became gradually stronger as I aged and reached their highest strength when I was around the age of twenty-five years old. The hallucinations finally became less frequent as I matured. I am completely at their mercy. When they strike, I can do nothing but surrender to them.

While I was living and working in Paris in 1883, a well-known French businessman in manufacturing invited me along to an expedition, and I gladly took him up on the offer. I had been spending entirely too much time working in dusty factories. I was thrilled to explore nature.

The adventure had a deep effect on me. Usually, that would be a good thing, but soon my brain was buzzing anxiously with too many thoughts. Soon, it became much worse. **On my return to the city that night, I felt a positive sensation that my brain had caught fire. I saw a light as though a small sun was located in it and I passed the whole night applying cold compressions to my tortured head.** The flashes from this episode did not relent for almost a month and when I was invited to their next expedition, my answer was a stern and fast "No thank you."

**These luminous phenomena still manifest themselves from time to time, as when a new idea opening up possibilities strikes me, but they are no longer exciting, being of relatively small intensity. When I close my eyes, I invariably observe first a background of very dark and uniform blue, not unlike the sky on a clear but starless night. In a few seconds, this field**

becomes animated with innumerable scintillating flakes of green, arranged in several layers and advancing towards me. Then there appears, to the right, a beautiful pattern of two systems of parallel and closely spaced lines, at right angles to one another, in all sorts of colors with yellow, green, and gold predominating.

Just afterward, the lines become brighter and the entire scene becomes engulfed with tiny specks of flickering starlight dancing together in a thick crowd. The scene moves from the left side of my field of vision to the right until it fades away completely after ten seconds or so, leaving only a gray backdrop, until the images repeat themselves for another round. When I lay in bed to sleep, this is what I see every night.

If I close my eyes for long enough, I eventually see images of people and objects appearing in my vision at some point after the lightshow. This is always an indication that I am just about to fall asleep. If people and objects do not make an appearance, I know I am in for a night of bad sleep.

\* \* \*

I was an ordinary child, for the most part. Like many children, I wished that I could fly. Sometimes a powerful wind would blow from the nearby mountains, and I would jump into the air, pretending I was shooting upwards through the sky. As I grew older, it was upsetting to reach the point when I could no longer trick myself into thinking I was actually flying.

Throughout my childhood, I developed some peculiar likes and dislikes, and some truly strange habits. **I had a violent aversion against the earrings of women, but other ornaments, as bracelets, pleased me more or less according to design. The sight of a pearl would almost give me a fit, but I was fascinated with the glitter of crystals or objects with sharp edges and plane surfaces.**

**I would not touch the hair of other people except, perhaps at the point of a revolver.** The sight of a peach would make me feel sick, and the smell of turpentine oil would make me want to crawl out of my skin. When I would line baking pans with parchment for my mother, I would always feel a disgusting taste in my mouth. I don't know why.

I would count every step I took as I was walking from place to place. I made mental calculations to guess the cubical volume of soup, coffee cups, and items of food in a meal. I couldn't enjoy eating until I had done this first. **All repeated acts or operations I performed had to be divisible by three and if I missed, I felt impelled to do it all over again, even if it took hours. I was oppressed by thoughts of pain in life and death and religious fear. I was swayed by superstitious belief and lived in constant dread of the spirit of evil, of ghost and ogres and other unholy monsters of the dark.**

At around the age of twelve, I was at the very height of my shyness. I lacked even the smallest properties of courage that any given person should possess. I was constantly a victim of my own fear until, suddenly, the entire course of my existence was altered.

I began to love books above all other things. My father had a beautiful and spacious library, and If I ever saw any chance to enter it, I would walk softly and sneak inside. That library was my very first view of heavenly bliss, but my father became a tyrant if he caught me reading his books. I was not allowed in the library.

**He hid the candles when he found that I was reading in secret,** and he gave me a stern warning that reading in the dark would spoil my eyes and cause blindness.

I was clever when faced with this predicament. I watched my mother craft many items, and I knew that I could make useful things if I needed them, too. So I took to building my own candles.

I found the animal fat I needed, I made a wick, and I melded the animal fat around the wick with a cast made of tin. I would sneak into the library and cover the cracks of the doors so that light wouldn't show through to the other side. I read until dawn or until I heard my mother stirring to start her daily farm labors, both of which were my signals to retreat from the forbidden library.

One book in particular had a deep impression on me. It was a work by the well-known Hungarian novelist, Josika, in my native Serbian translation. This book first made me aware of ideas like honor and duty. After reading it I began to practice self-control, or at least as much as a child could do such a thing. I failed miserably at first, but eventually I began to succeed in the little childhood goals I set for myself. I swelled with nationalism and pride for doing so, thinking of myself as a strong Serbian man of honor.

Over the course of my life, I continued practicing self-control and of living a life with honor. Through discipline, it has become my nature to exercise caution and control in all things. I do not mean to say that I am immune to temptation or that I am more pure than any other person. I merely strive to be good, even though we are all born into sin.

As I gained maturity, the usual human desires emerged from inside of me. Temptation always won in the beginning, but I eventually conquered each and every vice as they developed. Sin would swell up from inside of me and render me powerless over it. I would choose virtue, defeating my vices through willpower and persistence. This sort of battle is never truly won, but with intention, persistence, and frequent repentance, wellness is maintained.

During my twenties, I deviated the most. I succumbed to drinking too much alcohol and smoking too many cigarettes. I was confident in my ability to do no wrong, but **after years of discipline, I gained so complete a mastery**

**over myself that I toyed with passions which have meant destruction to some of the strongest men.** I fell deeply into my vices as a young man, and they consumed me. It was years before I realized that I had strayed at all.

As a boy, I thought I had so much control over myself that I could not possibly be corrupted. I was proven wrong when, still in college, I developed a true madness for gambling. It was my first addiction and vice. **To sit down to a game of cards was for me the quintessence of pleasure.**

My father, a priest and a man who lived life as an example to others, could not forgive this senseless act that was a clear waste of money—especially when I was disciplined by the school for my behavior. My reasoning was terrible. I would say to him, "I don't have a problem, and I can quit whenever I wish! Why not enjoy myself? What can be the harm?"

My father and I would get into big fights over this, but my mother had a different approach. She had a better understanding of human nature. She knew that a person could only change if they so desired. One day, when I had lost all of my money from playing cards and was itching for another round, my mother handed me a thick roll of bills and spoke these words, **"Go and enjoy yourself. The sooner you lose all we possess, the better it will be. I know that you will get over it."**

After hearing these sobering words, I did get over it. My mother's strategy worked brilliantly. From that moment on, I have lived my life with just as much desire to gamble as I have for pulling out my own teeth. I never played a single game of cards again.

Around the same time, I developed a terrible habit of smoking. When my health began to deteriorate, I evoked my best willpower and was able to quit completely. On another occasion, after experiencing heart problems and discovering that the culprit was my daily morning cup of coffee, I quit that habit as well. These were difficult habits to curb, I must profess. In my life I have come across other bad habits that have come and gone.

I think it is necessary to take joy in having personal responsibility. The self-control that others might call sacrifice brings me joy and freedom. Abstinence from the natural desires is not always my preference, but I find that the rewards always outweigh the struggle. Many times in my life, I have endured sicknesses of life-threatening quality. Despite this, even at an elderly age I am in excellent health from living with good habits.

Just recently I was returning to my home at the Waldorf-Astoria Hotel. That night, the New York City air was frigid, and gusts of freezing air were flinging rain and sleet into my face from all directions. The ground was slippery with ice, making it difficult to walk. I could find no taxi to hail. I hurried home and noticed a man about a block behind me who seemed just as eager to escape the terrible weather.

My feet slipped on the ground. Without warning my legs came high into the air. At my body's impulses, I spun 180 degrees in mid-air and landed safely on my hands and feet. I recovered and continued walking home. The man behind me hurried to see if I was all right. Astonished, he asked me how old I was. "Ah, close to fifty-nine," I joked. "Why do you ask?" "Why," he spoke, **"I have seen a cat do this, but never a man."**

On another recent occasion, I wanted to have new eye glasses created and made a trip to see the eye-glass maker. He had me read from the usual charts at a distance, and I read all the tiniest letters. He looked at me with suspicion when I told him I was more than sixty years old. **Friends of mine often remark**

**that my suits fit me like gloves but they do not know that all my clothing was made to measurements which were taken nearly fifteen years ago and never changed.** My size and weight have not changed the tiniest bit. That reminds me of a great story, actually.

It was the winter of 1885. I was on a night out in the company of Mr. Edison and some of his executives at the Edison Illuminating Company. We went to enjoy ourselves at a place across the street from the company offices located at 65th Avenue. One gentleman suggested we have a game of guessing each other's weight, so we gathered around a scale to begin the games.

Edison looked at me from top to bottom with a squint in his eye and said, **"Tesla weighs 152 lbs. to an ounce,"** and he guessed it exactly. Stripped I weighed 142 pounds, and that is still my weight.** I leaned in toward the ear of Edward H. Johnson to ask him discreetly, **"How is it possible that Edison could guess my weight so closely?"**

**"Well,"** he said, lowering his voice. **"I will tell you confidentially, but you must not say anything. He was employed for a long time in a Chicago slaughter-house where he weighed thousands of hogs every day. That's**

**why."** Very often we hear jokes, but weeks pass before we truly understand them. Then we laugh out loud much later for the first time of getting the joke. I must admit it took me longer than a year to comprehend Mr. Johnson's joke.

I say again, my exemplary health is the calculated effect of many years of living with meticulous attention towards well-being. The most curious thing out of this is that many times in my life as a young man, I was completely overtaken by serious health conditions that made me **a hopeless physical wreck and given up by physicians.** As if that was not enough, through foolishness, I've put myself into quite a few life-threatening situations and somehow made it out alive.

As a youth, I almost drowned, I was trapped, I was lost, and another time frozen. I **had hair-breadth escapes from mad dogs, hogs, and other wild animals.** I allowed myself to come into contact with deadly diseases and found myself involved with all sorts of misfortunates time and time again throughout my youth. In each case, I escaped death's grasp. Looking back on all of these dangerous instances, I am certain my survival was not by coincidence. I almost think my survival must have been made possible by divine intervention.

It is not much of a stretch to say that the inventor's job is to save lives. If the inventor is generating electrical power, improving existing devices, or adding new conveniences, that person is, in essence, making life safer. Inventors are also better suited than most people to protect themselves in dangerous situations because of their creative and clever nature. If I had not known about my creativity as an inventor, I would know about my cleverness from responding to these dangerous experiences.

Once I was on a swimming trip to a lake when I was fourteen years old. I decided to scare my friends. The plan was simple: I would dive under a long boardwalk and sneak out at the other end to surprise them. **Swimming and diving came to me as naturally as a duck, and I was confident that I could perform the feat.** When I saw that my friends weren't looking, I dove underneath the boardwalk.

After swimming underwater for what seemed like several minutes, I came up for air. To my surprise, I found a solid barrier blocking the way. I remained calm and focused, and pushed myself off of the structure to gain speed. I moved faster until my lungs could not bear another moment without a breath. When I arose for the second time to look for an escape, I was trapped. At that moment, I became frantic.

I gathered all of my remaining energy and made a third, desperate attempt to find a way out. The torment of not being able to breathe was insufferable. My mind was fading. My sight was going dark. Surely all hope was lost. I was not moving, and my body was slowly gliding downward. In that moment, I experienced a vision of flashing light. The blinding jolt snapped me back and saved me from an impending death.

Suddenly, I realized there was a tiny space between the surface of the water and the wooden structure above it. With hardly any life left in me, I rose up and pressed my lips against the wooden boards. Along with air, I took in a small amount of water. I nearly choked to death.

I did this for several moments until my fast beating heart slowed pace. By this time, my state of consciousness was in a dreamlike trance, fully aware of the danger I was in but at peace with my surroundings. I didn't have enough oxygen to think clearly. Perhaps I was running on pure instinct in the moments that followed. Once my heartbeat returned to a normal rhythm, I gained control of myself.

I continued to look for a way out. I had lost my sense of direction and couldn't remember where I had come from. However, after many tries I finally made it out. My friends were glad to see me alive after that. I avoided swimming for the rest of the year, but somehow I didn't properly learn my lesson.

Two years later, I came to find myself in an even worse situation while swimming in the water. There was a dam outside the city where I attended school, and it was built alongside a river. As a safety ordinance, the recommended water level was two or three inches above the height of the dam. I thought it was not dangerous to swim near the dam. I did it regularly.

One day I went into the river alone for a swim. Suddenly, I found myself being pulled toward the edge of the dam. Knowing it was a long fall below the dam, I screamed. The water was much higher than usual, and my body shot quickly towards the edge.

I tried to swim away from the edge of the dam, but it was too late. The current had me in a tight grip. With both hands, I reached downward and grabbed the tip of the dam before I was carried off. My feet were now dangling behind me as the water was pushing me forcefully towards certain death. I struggled to keep a grip and it was difficult to breathe. The muscles in my neck strained to keep my head above water. I screamed for help, but no one could hear me. The loud raging falls drowned out the sounds of my cries.

My whole body was shaking as I held on for dear life. If I were to let go, I would fall onto the jagged rocks below. A flash of light appeared before me in my panic. I left the world around me, seeing only a whirling, piercing light. In my vision, I saw a diagram from one of my textbooks. I remembered that the surface area acted upon was proportionate to the force being applied. Instinctively, I turned with my left side facing forward. **As if by magic, the pressure was reduced and I found it comparatively easy in that position to resist the force of the stream.** It was suddenly half as difficult to hold on, but I was not out of danger yet.

I was still trapped, and the force of the water would eventually carry me to my death. I was left-handed at the time, and my right arm was especially weak. Switching to my right side would have been a grave mistake. My only option was to slowly nudge myself along the wall of the dam. Inch by inch, I made my way towards the edge to find a way out.

The current was strong. I trudged along, holding myself to the dam as I moved. My muscles ached, and my skin stung from the force of the water. I almost didn't make it because of a dip in the stone wall towards the end. Mustering up the last of my strength, I finally pulled myself to dry land. I let out a cry of relief before falling unconscious in the nearby grass.

Later, some of the townsfolk found me, and I was given medical attention. The left side of my body was red, swollen, and itchy. I had a fever for weeks. The pain rendered my left arm useless. Therefore, I trained myself to use my right hand and became ambidextrous. **These are only two of many instanced, but they may be sufficient to show that had it not been for the inventor's instinct, I would not have lived to tell the tale.**

I am very often asked how I came to be a famous inventor and at what age did I begin to show an interest in inventing. One of my earliest recollections of the act of invention took place when a boyhood pal acquired a fishing hook with some tackle, creating a buzz among other boys in the village. We all wanted hooks of our own after seeing his.

The next day, all the boys met to share the one hook and catch frogs together for sport. I sat out on all of this fun because of a silly childhood disagreement with the boy. We weren't getting along at that particular time. I had never seen a hook before, but the idea of one seemed exciting. I searched through my parents' tools, found some thin iron wire and hammered it into a sharp point. Then I bent it into a round shape and tied wire onto it. I fashioned a rod, found some bait, and walked over to the stream where there was no shortage of frogs.

I tried to catch a frog but failed. I was about to walk back home when I saw a nice, plump frog sitting directly in the middle of a large tree stump. After several failed attempts to catch the frog, I wondered what would happen if I used the hook without bait. Initially, the frog reared back as if to hide. Then its eyes swelled up out of their sockets to twice their original size, and it pounced toward the hook. I had caught my first frog.

I tried this method on two other frogs. It worked each time. I had become a master frog catcher! Meeting up with my companions later, I discovered they were empty-handed. Like the frogs, they were green with envy. At first, I didn't allow anyone to know my secret. I enjoyed being the king of the frog catchers. Eventually, I didn't have the heart to keep my friends in the dark. I showed them my simple trick. When summer came again, the boys in my village brought a massacre to the frogs.

My second showing of inventive prowess much more resembled that of my later engineering career. It is a funny story having to do with May bugs, or June bugs as they are named in the United States. In my homeland, May bugs are such a terrible pest that they commonly break entire tree branches with their weight. I can tell you, they are a real problem.

I made something much like a small turbine or windmill. I produced a small wooden cross with each end being of the same length just like a plus sign. With my parents' drill, I made a hole in the center of the cross so that a dowel stick could fit through and in between a spindle so that it could spin.

Now, here is where the bugs came into play. It was easy finding the bugs, **the bushes were black with them.** I would catch four bugs at a time and tie one to each end of the turbine in order for the turbine to spin and produce power. In their attempts to fly away, the bugs caused the turbine to spin. The bugs were fantastic for this and kept the fan spinning for hours. Subsequently, I attached the turbine to another disk, and to my pleasure, witnessed the transfer of power to the outer disk.

This outdoor childhood experiment went on blissfully until one day, a very stupid and disgusting boy came to taunt me. The little monster grabbed the bugs off of my turbine, tossed them into his mouth as if they were escargot, all the while laughing like a brute. **That disgusting sight terminated my endeavors in this promising field, and I have never since been able to touch a May bug or any other insect for that matter.**

Nevertheless, I kept exploring new promising fields of interest. For example, I started a project using some of my grandfather's old clocks that I had found in a storage barn. I intended to take apart the clocks and put them back together. However, I was only successful at taking them apart. My mother spanked me for breaking the clocks.

Soon after that, I made a very fun pop-gun out of a hollow tube and some hemp for the plugs. The trick was finding the right tube with enough strength from the hollow stalks that grew in our garden. It was a fine pop-gun and made a perfectly loud pop sound when shot. It could shoot a good distance also. I did, however, shoot out some window panes by mistake. My mother spanked twice as hard for breaking the window.

If I remember the order of everything correctly, my next inventive activity was to craft swords. I used pieces of furniture and carved them into the right shape with a nice point. I was still deeply influenced by the Serbian literature I had been reading and I especially loved heroes and acts of bravery in battle. With sword in hand, I played the hero. The corn stalks in our garden field were my enemies, all of whom I conquered like a true warrior. For all of this, I received the most brutal corporal punishment out of all my childhood by my mother's hand. I had toyed with the May bugs, clocks, pop-gun, and swords, all before the age of six.

Right around that time, my family moved from the countryside village of Smiljan to the nearby small city of Gospic. **This change of residence was like a calamity to me. It almost broke my heart to part from our pigeons, chickens and sheep, and our magnificent flock of geese which used to rise to the clouds in the morning and return from the feeding grounds at sundown in battle formation, so perfect that it would have put a squadron of the best aviators of the present day to shame.** I no longer had free rein over the fields and forest, and no longer was the open air my kingdom. Now I was trapped in a new house with nothing to do but to peek outside the blinds to watch strangers pass as I filled with anxiety. **My bashfulness was such that I would rather have faced a roaring lion than one of the city dudes who strolled about.**

At eight years old, the hardest part about the transition to Gospic was the weekly trip to a new church. Every Sunday it was my nightmare to put on my Sunday best and have to face the townsfolk. I don't think I once made eye contact with anyone at church. I remember feeling my heart beating in my throat as I crossed through those grand double doors week after week. This was because soon after moving to Gospic, I had made a fool out of my-self at church. Ever since that incident, I felt the same embarrassment whenever I was in church.

One Sunday, I had just finished my duty of ringing the church bells and I flew down the stairs. I felt playful and joyful, as every child does when the sermon is over and church lets out. I could go outside, scream with joy and swing my arms and do as I pleased. When I reached the outdoors I saw a rich lady, lavishly dressed, followed by a group of personal attendants who carried the long tail of her dress.

I'm not sure if this was ever fashionable in America, but at the time it was normal to see a formidable woman in Europe with a dress that extended in the back with fabric trailing behind her at what would now be considered a comical distance. I saw a few men carrying the back of her dress, and decided in an in-stant that I should jump right in the center of them. I did exactly this and tore a great rip in the long garment as I screamed trium-phantly.

It was the most angry I had ever seen my father. **He gave me a gentle slap on the cheek, the only corporal punishment he ever**

**administered to me, but I almost feel it now.** It was the public humiliation that hurt more than the actual slap.

Just moments before I was on high, and now I was utterly confused and tormented. I felt like nobody liked me. Maybe it was my imagination, but I was sure that everyone in the town was avoiding me after that day. This feeling persisted until one glorious event, when I earned back my esteem within the community.

**An enterprising young merchant had organized a fire department. A new fire engine was purchased, uniforms provided, and the men drilled for service and parade.** Everyone was talking about how great it would be to see the parade. I sat and watched the ceremony, during which the fire department was going to conduct the first official test of the water hose.

The entire town and some from neighboring villages came to the event. A few hundred people had gathered to watch the new fire engine in action. With a fresh coat of red and black paint, the vehicle led the parade. At the ceremony that followed, the new fire captain gave the order for his men to engage the water pump. I was in the crowd watching as the firemen stood in line, clutching onto the hose.

To everyone's surprise, not a single drop of water came out of the hose.

Local professors and others tried unsuccessfully to find the problem. By that time, the excitement in the crowd had burned out. Nevertheless, I offered to help solve the problem. I didn't know anything about how to operate a hose or a pump, and I was absolutely ignorant of air pressure and basic physics. I didn't know anything about working with machines at all. However, my gut told me to feel around in the water for the suction hose, where I found the problem.

In the river, up to my chest in water, I discovered that the hose had buckled. I dove below the surface of the water, pulled on the hose, and brought it back into working condition. Then POOF! Water sprayed everywhere as the gigantic hose jerked each and every way like a snake in the air. The crowd went wild with enthusiasm, and the entire city cheered for me. A group of men picked me up by the waist and passed me from one set of shoulders to another. They carried me all around the square. As a result, I had a much better experience with the people in Gospic from that day forward.

Not long after moving into the city, my parents enrolled me into the preparatory school for young boys at the Real Gymnasium, where my childhood adventures resumed. As with my stunt with frogs at Smiljan, I established myself here as the top man in the art of catching crows. It was quite easily done, too. I would hide in the bushes, make myself small, and impersonate a bird call. Then, birds would answer back with their own call.

Soon, I would hear the flapping of wings and see a crow landing near my hiding spot. I would toss a stick in another direction to distract the bird's attention, then quickly grab its body. I could easily catch as many birds as I wanted doing this, but one day the birds fought back.

At the time, I was with a friend, walking home after catching two beautiful crows. Suddenly, we noticed hundreds of crows gathering around us. The birds loomed over us in the sky like dark storm clouds. As we walked further, they landed on nearby tree branches in our path. They quickly had us completely surrounded. The birds let out an awful howl and we realized we were in genuine danger. **All of the sudden, I received a blow on the back of my head, which knocked me down.**

As I fell to the ground, birds from every direction pecked at my flesh. I let go of my prized bird in an instant to shield my face from their attacks. We struggled with the birds for a moment more, but once they recovered their loved-ones, they quickly retreated. I had learned my lesson. I would never again take sport with catching a crow.

As a young boy in school, I was fascinated with water turbines. After reading about Niagara Falls, I imagined a great big wheel harnessing power from the falls. I built many small models and tested them in the local streams. My water turbines were completely operational. I loved these toys.

My uncle didn't like my hobby. He told me to stop wasting my time with "those silly turbines." I shot right back at him, proclaiming that one day I would build a turbine at Niagara Falls. My uncle scoffed at me. Thirty years later, I designed and built turbines at Niagara Falls that powered all of New York. I was the first to harness the power of the falls, turning it into electricity. The joy of having carried out a childhood dream that large is inexpressible.

During childhood, I built several contraptions, the best of which by far was my crossbow. It was the ultimate toy. I would go to the edge of the city and shoot arrows into the forest. My crossbow could fling arrows so far that they would vanish into the horizon. If my parents had known what I was doing, they would have been furious.

My second favorite toy I built was a slingshot. I practiced with it constantly. One afternoon, I was walking along the river with my uncle. Trout were jumping up from the water. I looked to my uncle and said, "Not only will I be able to hit one of the jumping fish, but I can cut the fish clean in half."

I took aim and released my grip. The rock shot out and hit a fish, and the two halves of its body fell back into the river. It was a trick I had practiced many times. My uncle walked away from me and called me a devil. He did not speak to me for weeks. I often look back at that moment and remember who I once was at that very young age.

# PART THREE

I was ten years old when I enrolled at the prep school at the Real Gymnasium. Being a new building, the science departments were stocked with shiny new microscopes, flasks, tubes, and all the other equipment needed to teach growing minds. I was captivated by every experiment our instructors would carry out. This excitement was critical for leading me down the path of becoming a great inventor.

I loved the brain-teasing puzzles from my math classes. The teachers applauded my speed at completing equations, because I was the fastest in class. It was thrilling to compete with the other classmates, but I had an unfair advantage. I could hallucinate the numbers at will, seeing them suspended in the air wherever I wished. This method was much faster than writing the numbers out on paper. I was unbeatable.

Although I was an expert at solving equations, my handwriting was awful, and my drawing was even worse. At school, we were required to draw freehand in some classes. I struggled with these assignments. It was absolute torture for me to sit and draw. When it was time to submit my work to the teacher, I would go into a frenzy, becoming hot and red in the face. Despite having top skills in math, my shortcomings with a pen and parchment nearly caused me to fail in school. **Had it not been for a few exceptionally stupid boys, who could not do anything at all, my record would have been the worst.**

Although I had some struggles at school, my imagination continued to thrive. For example, my triumph with the fire engine pump had left me obsessed with the idea of a vacuum. During the year that followed the fire engine parade, I thought of ways to build a perpetual motion machine by using a vacuum. According to the laws of physics, a perpetual motion machine is impossible. Nevertheless, I've always loved to challenge the impossible.

Experimenting with an idea, I attached two wooden ball bearings underneath a cylinder, which I encased in an air-tight container. The container had two separate compartments, and the cylinder was connected to both of them, divided by sliding joints that were air-tight. I had fooled myself into thinking that I had actually succeeded, and at that point I took to applying my idea for creating a flying machine.

At that age I had also spent a lot of time jumping off from high places, slowing my fall with a large umbrella for a parachute. After a bad fall with the umbrella, I had decided to halt these activities. But now I had a perpetual motion machine, or so I thought, and it occurred to me that I should use it to provide infinite power to a new flying machine. In theory, the cylinder from the perpetual motion machine would act as the rotating shaft underneath the flying machine, like that of an automobile.

It was a bitter realization once I realized the perpetual motion machine did not work. The cylinder had maintained extra spin from an air leak in the container, and for a while I thought the contraption was working perfectly. It was a good try, but the machine was useless. According to the first and second laws of thermodynamics, a perpetual motion machine is impossible. In essence, I had tested those laws and had learned to respect them. This kind of thinking eventually led me to accomplishing feats that other people called impossible.

Just after graduating school at the Real Gymnasium, I became terribly ill for some unknown reason. My head throbbed with pain, and I had very little energy. My body felt like it was weighed down with a blanket of lead. I struggled to stand upright. Because doctors didn't know how to treat me, I was left with the option to rest in bed. Though the pain was awful, I had the advantage of unlimited time for reading.

On days when I felt strong enough to stand, I made trips to the public library, where I developed friendships with library staff. I didn't finish my goal, but I had the intention of reading every last book in the building. One day, a staff member led me into a locked room that contained books which had not yet been categorized. They told me I could read any book I wished. I volunteered my time to organize the books into the public shelves where they belonged.

During one of my trips to the library, the staff gave me a stack of storybooks written by a new American author, Mark Twain. Not since reading Serbian epics as a young child had I become so enamored by an author's writing. Immersed in these tales of life in the American South, I forgot about the pain in my body. You may think I'm crazy, but I believe reading these stories restored my health.

Although I haven't gambled in decades, I would be willing to bet that medical science will one day discover the close connection between the mind and the body. Mood and outlook are essential for maintaining good health. I bet a happy person can recover from an illness more quickly than a miserable person with the same illness.

Twain's stories lifted my spirit, and my body recovered completely. Later in my life, I was blessed to meet Samuel Clemens, who writes under the pseudonym of Mark Twain. I told him his stories had transformed my life. From that day forward, we remained dear friends.

After I recovered from my illness, my parents enrolled me into a secondary school that was a long distance from home. I was relocated to live with my aunt in Carlstadt, where I could be close to the school. My aunt was a refined woman. Her husband was a colonel who had survived many horrors of battle.

**I can never forget the three years I passed at their home. No fortress in time of war was under a more rigid discipline. I was fed like a canary bird.** Although my aunt's cooking was the best I had ever eaten, the portions she served were smaller than a military ration. **The slices of ham cut by my aunt were like tissue paper.** Sometimes, the colonel would drop a thick, hot omelet onto my plate. My aunt would seize the food before I could even react. **"Be careful, Niko is very delicate,"** she would tell him. If by delicate she meant hungry, then I very much was so.

Although I felt like I was slowly starving while living with my aunt and uncle, there was something remarkable about their home. **I lived in an atmosphere of refinement and artistic taste quite unusual for those times and conditions.** Living with them was my first exposure to a type of class and appreciation for culture that I would often encounter in my adulthood, as I moved into the larger cities. Although I appreciated the opportunity to live with my aunt and uncle, there were reasons I wanted to leave. The food shortage was the least of our problems.

The area was swarming with nasty insects. My body quickly became infected with malaria. Although I drank medicine every day, my fever persisted. Another problem was periodic flooding due to rain. Whenever the town experienced flooding, every home and building fell victim to waves of rats. The townsfolk tried unsuccessfully to ward off the rats with large bundles of paprika. The smell of the spice was such that it would have driven out the most stubborn of men, but it had no effect on the rats.

After the town's attempt to eradicate the rats failed, I stepped in to solve the problem. After all, I was skilled at catching small animals. Soon, I became known throughout town as the rat-catching boy. I don't know what was worse, the starvation, the malaria, or being called the rat-catching boy.

To my relief, I finished school and returned to my parents' home. As much as I wanted to leave Carlstadt, problems awaited me at home. When it was time for me to return home, I knew my parents would pressure me to enter the priesthood.

I was unsure of how to proceed with this problem. For the sake of my family's reputation, they would have also found it acceptable for me to choose a career in the military, but I wanted to avoid that just as well. The slim list of available options was also the reason my parents pushed me in the direction of the clergy. I had developed so much of a passion for electricity that I knew I couldn't go forward with the life they had chosen for me. I wanted to study electricity.

The infatuation had grown much during my time at secondary school in Carlstadt. My professor of physics had been particularly exciting. He would build machines to demonstrate concepts during class. His lectures weren't just words, they were living commands that turned ideas into action. "Like this," he would say, connecting a wire from a machine to a battery. Moving parts came alive through the use of electricity as a result. For me, it was like witnessing a miracle. I yearned for a life in which I could spend most of my time playing with electricity.

Ultimately, I accepted my fate for otherwise. I readied myself for the journey home to greet and begin this new life. Just days before my departure, however, I was handed a letter from my father. He wanted me to join him for a hunting trip far outside Gospic. It was inconsistent with his character, because he had always been against such activities. Soon after receiving the letter, news was spreading that cholera had swept over my homeland. I made a rash decision to disobey my father's request and travel directly back home.

**I contracted the disease on the very day of my arrival.** No doubt I was susceptible, having recently recovered from malaria. The cholera quickly infected me, taking command over my body.

Every twenty years or so, the cholera would spread throughout our country. The people of Gospic, until recently, would burn powerful incense to kill off the disease. It is a shame we didn't know the disease came from infected drinking water. Many people in my country had died from cholera. Luckily, I survived, but I went through nine months of sheer agony.

During those months of illness, I was confined to my bed. Whenever I stood, I would become dizzy and lose my sense of balance. In which case, I would quickly find my way into bed again. One night, my symptoms grew worse. My mother leapt to retrieve my father, thinking I would die at any moment.

During those months, I felt a sensation that my head was being squeezed tightly. That night in particular, it was like my face had been beaten in a boxing match. Sweat poured out of me as I gasped for air. My parents returned to the room, and my father stood over me. **I still see his pallid face as he tried to cheer me in tones belying his assurance.**

**"Perhaps," I said, "I may get well if you will let me study engineering."** Squeezing my hands tightly, my father told me I would go to the best schools in the world. Miraculously, the next day, word of a new medicine began spreading throughout town. I quickly recovered after regular doses of the new medicine. It was an awful tasting elixir made from some sort of bean, but it saved my life.

Recovering from cholera, I was painfully skinny. It was my father's idea that I rehabilitate myself by spending the next year hiking in the mountain wilderness. I carried only the essential gear as well as some books. It did my body well, and in my time spent there I came up with many ideas. Finally, my mind was free to think about engineering with the luxury of knowing I could actually study the subject. I thought of so many ideas. Some of the ideas are silly to me, now that I am more educated, but thinking big is always a good place to start.

One idea I had was for a pressurized tube that would transport packages and letters across the ocean. Another fantastical idea of mine was to build a mega-sized ring that circled the entire globe as a transportation system. The idea was to create something much faster than railroad transportation. It might be impossible to build something like that, but it's a fun idea.

A very important idea struck me on these hikes. It occurred to me that potential electrical energy was surrounding all things, everywhere. **We are whirling through endless space with an inconceivable speed. All around us everything is spinning, everything is moving, everywhere is energy. There must be some way of availing ourselves of this energy more directly.**

Most of us know the story of Newton's apple in relation to gravity, so I will use an apple to give an example. When an apple sits completely still on a branch, it remains spinning along with its surroundings through the rotational force of Earth's spinning axis. Every still object we see is somehow in motion. If there was somehow a way to collect the cosmic energy being applied to ordinary objects all around us, that rotational energy from a single, still apple could be enough energy to make a crater in the Earth the size of the Grand Canyon. Perhaps more. If it could even be done, that same energy could also provide electric power to the masses. **The mere contemplation of these magnificent possibilities expands our minds, strengthens our hopes, and fills our hearts with supreme delight.**

After a year of hiking in the mountains, my body had fully recovered. Finally, it was time to begin my university education in engineering. I left my parents' home once again to travel to the city of Gratz in the land of Styria,[3] where I would study at the poly-technic school there. My father had delivered on his word that I would go to the best schools, and he had picked this one himself.

I woke early every day at three o'clock to begin work, and I studied until eleven in the night. This included weekends. I was motivated to become the best electrician that ever lived. It had been my longing to study engineering since I was a small child and finally, there I was. I did not take this opportunity for granted. I worked day and night, studying

---

[3] Now spelled Graz. Styria is a province in southeast Austria.

furiously. My parents would be so proud, I thought.

I had an advantage over the other students because I read more books than they, even before the courses began. I studied without rest, and by no surprise, my progress stood far above all the others. After the first year, I had excelled to a point that my professors had never seen in a student. That summer when I returned home, I was grief-stricken when my father didn't acknowledge my hard work. I showed him my papers and told him stories of praise I had received from my teachers, but he said almost nothing.

**That almost killed my ambition; but later, after he had died, I was pained to find a package of letters which the professors had written to him to the effect that unless he took me away from the institution I would be killed through overwork.** The following year, I began to loosen up on myself in my work ethic. I was still highly devoted to learning all things related to mechanical physics, but I began to relax and enjoy myself some. Instead of spending all my waking hours working, I would split my time between studying and reading in the library for fun.

Once I found a book I liked, I simply couldn't put it down. I had picked up a piece written by Voltaire and was helplessly caught in his writing like a fish on a hook. There was no escape. I decided I would read every word that Voltaire had written, which amounted to almost one hundred books, all with thick spines. While I studied in Gratz, I read every last one of them.

My extreme dedication during my first year had gained me close relationships to many of my professors. Dr. Alle, in particular, closely observed my education. **This scientist was the most brilliant lecturer to whom I ever listened.** He would stay with me in the lecture room for hours after class, giving me problems to solve.

Dr. Alle was very supportive of all the ideas I expressed to him, no matter how big or impossible they seemed. Professor Poeschl was another professor with whom I held a close relationship, but he did not always offer the same support for my idealism. **Professor Poeschl was a methodical and thoroughly grounded German. All of his experiments were skillfully performed with clock-like precision and without a miss.** One instance with Poeschl in particular made a lasting impression in my mind. It is something I often think back to, especially on a bad day when I need to cheer myself.

It was in my second year at the poly-technic school when this incident occurred. That year, the institution acquired a Gramme machine. It was an early type of electrical generator with a giant magnet and big hand-crank. During a lecture, Professor Poeschl was running the machine. Sparks flew out in all directions. All machinery from that period had an inherent design flaw. As a result, much of the applied electrical energy was wasted as sparks escaped from the machine's metal brushes. It was the first successful electrical generator used for commercial use. It was new at the time, but very crude and inefficient. Now an antique.

I watched as the sparks whizzed from the machine, and I immediately thought: surely there is a better way. I spoke up in the lecture hall that day to suggest that a motor could be made using fewer components, resulting in a better machine. No sparks. No wasted energy.

He paused the demonstration to make a point of teasing me. **"Mr. Tesla may accomplish great things, but he certainly will never do this. It would be equivalent to converting a** steadily pulling force, like that of gravity, into a rotary effort. It is a perpetual motion scheme, an impossible idea." In front of the whole class, he dismissed my idea as silly. I would prove him wrong.

I respected my professor's skills in science, and for a while I submitted that his words must be the truth. My instinct continued to pull me back towards the idea of a better machine, however. Perhaps my subconscious mind knew something that my conscious mind did not. **Soon, I became convinced I was right and undertook the task with all the fire and boundless confidence of my youth.**

Using my ability to see things that aren't there, I began to imagine before me a machine whereby the electricity flowed by alternating currents, going back and forth. I turned the machine on and watched the currents circulate into the attached rotating coils. Next, I added an alternator into the machine and ran the simulation again to see how this change affected the run.

Then, I imagined a system of many generators working together to create electrical energy. Finally, I would rearrange the system and watch it play out in different ways. **The images I saw were to me perfectly real and**

**tangible.** I seemed so close to solving the problem of creating an alternating current machine. The rest of my time at the poly-technic school was spent obsessing over this idea.

I practically had the idea finished in theory, but a small part was missing and I couldn't put my finger on it. After obsessing for months, I began to think again that perhaps my professor was correct. Maybe alternating current was impossible to create after all.

I never finished university. Although I hold a stack of honorary doctorates with degrees from Columbia and Yale included, I never finished my courses at the poly-technic school at Gratz. In my third year, I became insufferably bored and restless.

I had read everything interesting that was in the libraries. The teachers had nothing left to teach me. I was so hungry for knowledge. I had been feeding myself a constant diet of knowledge for years and suddenly the plate was empty as I searched for more new things to learn. I was addicted to the feeling of learning new information. My teachers were giving lectures on subjects I had already read and re-read several times over. I couldn't focus in the lecture halls. I couldn't even pretend to care.

All I wanted to do was find a way to produce electricity through alternating currents.

There had to be a way to build a working Gramme machine that didn't eject sparks. It was all I could think about. There had to be a way to make such a machine of alternating electric currents. There just had to be a way. Very soon, I was in the habit of drinking too much wine. I smoked cigarettes almost constantly. One day, I decided to stop going to my lectures.

I was becoming increasingly frustrated with life in Gratz, so I went south to Maribor, Slovenia. There, I was able to find a job as a draftsman for an engineering company. It was something I could survive on, and I would take trips to my favorite pub there as often as I could. I paid very little attention to my work, but it was easy to maintain the job for a while.

I suppose I might have wasted my life drinking in Maribor for years if I had not been forced to leave. I lived in Slovenia for almost a full year until I was found by the authorities not to have a residence permit. I was detained and deported back to my family at Gospic, where I would stay for a brief visit.

My father was disappointed but relieved to see me. Facing him was difficult, and I felt regret for my decisions at our reunion. He told me I would finish my schooling in Prague. The term began soon, and I was to leave almost immediately so that I could attend registration.

I left, but I didn't make it in time. To make matters worse, upon my arrival I was told that in order to attend the school I was required to speak excellent Czech. I spoke some Czech, but not enough to please them. I wasn't able to enroll, but I was allowed to attend a few lectures while I waited on my admission status. Soon enough, my admission to the university was denied.

All these terrible things had been happening. There I was, distressed, having come full circle after throwing my life away recklessly and being given a second chance that I could not take. My family had intervened and put me back on track to earn a degree, and even then I had failed them. I suddenly felt so much shame for the burden I had become to my family. Yet, this idea of alternating current was all I could think about.

Then, an opportunity too good to be true suddenly appeared. In nearby Budapest, the first telephone systems in those parts of Europe were being planned. They would need someone with my knowledge and skills to work on these telephone systems. Lucky for me, a family friend held a high position in the company. When this job opportunity arose, I immediately left for Budapest.

I was under a lot of stress when I arrived in Budapest, so much so that I started seeing those erratic flashes of light I only see when I'm in extreme situations of great anxiety. I was fretfully worried about my life, my future, and upsetting my family yet again. I was a complete failure of a human being, and I was about to have to face my family again for it. Through all this, I still maintained my obsession with alternating current.

My anxieties crushed me, and I became ill. Once again, my body was crumbling. My senses failed me completely, and too much information was flowing through the brain. My eyes, ears, and all else were over-responsive. Like rapid fire, I was seeing blinding light radiating from every direction. An average sunny afternoon would have been enough to burst my brain. I was so sensitive to light that even with the curtains closed I could see very little other than a pounding white glow. I closed my eyes and the light burned into my skull through a barrage of other colors when I looked toward the windows from inside my home.

My nervous system was broken down completely. I could hear the ticking from a clock three rooms over. I could feel each tick like a hammer taken to the center of my skull. All around me were blinding white flashes, and the loud, low hum of everyday noise was so loud I couldn't bear it. I was in constant pain. With my hands clasped over my ears, I struggled to walk and see straight.

My muscles would twitch in regular spasms. Sometimes my whole body would shake without warning, and I had a fever. I tried to stay in my room because as soon as I walked out into the sunlight I was thrown into an out-of-body experience of pain and confusion. I sat in the darkness with a blanket over my head, enduring a frustrating inability to focus clearly.

Eventually I was cured, but not by the help of a medical practitioner. Someone did take me to see a man who, as I was told, was a great doctor. He said he had never seen a case like this before. He then instructed me to take large amounts of bromide of potassium twice a day and said there was nothing more he could do to help.

I have always wished that during that time, I had been supervised by true experts in psychology. It would have been marvelous to have people who could have devised ways to document some of the strange medical issues I've had throughout my life. I seem to be such a rare case.

My recovery was all thanks to a dear friend. This person was an athlete and knew well how both the body and mind can heal and grow stronger with diet and exercise. I wanted to feel better again, and so I pushed myself to follow the exercises he gave me. I had faced extreme illness too many times and I wouldn't let this be the end of me. After some weeks, my systems returned to normal function, and it was truly a miracle. Sight and sound, in particular, returned without distortion.

**My health returned and with it the vigor of mind.** This alternating current idea of mine consumed me completely for years, and again it was all I could think about. The idea was everything to me. By now, I had been looking to solve this problem for years. I couldn't find the answer yet, but the question echoed in my mind constantly. **Back in the deep recesses of the brain was the solution, but I could not yet give it outward expression.**

Suddenly, it came to me one day after I had recovered my health in Budapest. I was taking an afternoon stroll through the city park with a friend. The magnificent orange of the forming sunset reminded me of a passage of poetry. It is a favorite of mine that I have memorized, a passage from Goethe's *Faust*.

> *The glow retreats, done is the day of toil;*
> *It yonder hastes, new fields of life exploring;*
> *Ah, that no wing can lift me from the soil*
> *Upon its track to follow, follow soaring!*

My eureka moment came while I was reciting these lines. This time, no strange hallucinations, no mystical forces of nature, nor divine intervention came for me. The solution simply came into my mind after years of obsession. I reached to the ground to pick up a stick, and in the dirt I drew a diagram for what would later be my alternating magnetic field generator.

This invention would later usher the world into a new age of electricity. **A thousand secrets of nature which I might have stumbled upon accidentally, I would have given for that one which I had wrestled from her against all odds and at the peril of my existence.**

If this one invention was the only thing I had done with my life, it would have been enough. I had made it possible to safely distribute huge amounts of electricity across a large grid system, whereas small amounts of electricity could only be sent at a distance of roughly a mile before this machine existed. With this invention, I would one day power all of New York City, and the world.

# PART FOUR

After that wonderful day in the park, my mind began to swell with ideas. I threw all responsibilities into the wind and allowed myself the complete freedom to spend all of my hours imagining new machines. I was intoxicated with my own imagination, and **it was a mental state of happiness about as complete as I have ever known in my life.**

I sat and watched, all day long, picturing new devices as I put them together piece by piece in my imagination. I saw better turbines and engines than had ever been built in the past, all by my conception. I could see them all right in front of me, just as real to my eyes as the floor underneath me and the four walls that surrounded. I envisioned dozens of new machines.

The ideas came to me so quickly and naturally. The hardest part was retaining one idea to memory before another idea popped into existence and swayed all of my attention. So I sat there, endlessly thinking of new ideas and wrestling to maintain them all at once. **In less than two months, I evolved virtually all the types of motors and modifications of the system which are now identified with my name and many other names all over the world.**

I had come to live in Budapest at the high prospect of gaining employment, but it turned out that the telephone systems were not to be built for many months. Instead of working in the telephone business, I managed to find a job as a draftsman for the Central Telegraph Office maintained by the Hungarian government. I had plenty of experience. It didn't matter that I hated drafting, as the money they offered for the position would have likely been turned down by a more skilled draftsman.

The other talents that I did possess, however, earned me the respect of our chief of operations. Very quickly I was moved into the position of designing and installing new telegraph systems. When the first telephone finally arrived in Budapest, I then took the position of installing the telephones.

**The knowledge and practical experience I gained in the course of this work was the most valuable and the employment gave me ample opportunities for the exercise of my inventive**

**faculties.** I often had freedom in deciding how to constructively spend my time on the job and took to making a number of improvements on the machinery at the central telephone station. I also built a new amplifying speaker for telephone use that made it much easier to hear the person on the other side of the line. I never claimed rights to the invention, wrote, or spoke about it in public, but to this day that is the speaker used in telephones around the world.

**In recognition of my efficient assistance, the organizer of the undertaking, Mr. Puskas, upon disposing of business in Budapest, offered me a position in Paris which I gladly accepted.** I was thereafter employed in the Compagnie Continentale Edison, which of course was the French extension of Edison's company in America. I was delighted to serve Thomas Edison, by extension.

**I never can forget the deep impression that magic city produced on my mind. For several days after my arrival, I roamed through the streets in utter bewilderment of the spectacle.** I had never seen anything like it before. So many shops and places where people congregate! So much foot traffic! Fine coats and boots walked the streets at every turn.

Beautiful women everywhere, and romance in the air!

I had no ability to resist any of it. I became very adventurous when I first moved to Paris. Mister Puskas soon asked me how I was adjusting to the new city and I told him I was absolutely in love with the place. It would be much better still, I told him, if the city wasn't so expensive. **I described the situation accurately in the statement that "The last twenty-nine days of the month are the toughest."**

Once I settled into my work, my time in Paris was both busy and fulfilling. It was the point in my life when I was the most physically active. **Every morning, regardless of the weather, I would go from the Boulevard St. Marcel, where I resided, to a bathing house on the Seine; plunge into the water, loop the circuit twenty-seven times and then walk an hour to rich Ivry, where the company's factory was located. There I would have a wood-chipper's breakfast at half-past seven o'clock and then eagerly await the lunch hour, in the meanwhile cracking hard nuts for the manager of the works, Mr. Charles Bachelor, who was an intimate friend and assistant of Edison.**

Charles Bachelor was a lucky connection for me to have at that time. I had always admired Thomas Edison and Bachelor was not only a friend of Edison, but also his closest business partner. I even brushed shoulders with Edison once as he came to visit Paris to oversee his business. I felt very lucky at the time to have the opportunity to work for him, but in truth he was lucky to have me there to save his operations in Europe.

In Paris, I made some American friends as well. I got along so well with them at first chance, when we bonded over a game of pool. I was a decent pool player many years ago and won their admiration for it that evening. I told them about my invention for a machine that generates alternating current and how it could change the world.

One of the American men suggested that they and I team together to create a stock company. I laughed at the prospect. Nothing could have been a more outrageous idea to me. I did not have an understanding what this kind of offer entailed, **except that it was an American way of doing things.** We made no deals together. Just after meeting with them, it came to pass that I would spend the next months traveling to nearly every power plant in France and Germany on behalf of the Compagnie Continentale Edison to fix a mountain of problems and faulty wiring, with my own two hands.

After those few months of touring the region's power plants, I came back to Paris. I met with an administrator for the company and told him I could improve every electrical generator the company owned. He gladly gave me the clearance to make these adjustments and soon it was finished. The directors of the company were overjoyed that I had invented automatic regulators for the company's generators. Just after this, a big problem for the company arose.

A power plant had been built for the Germans on the French border town of Strasbourg. It was just outside the city along the railroad path to Germany. **The wiring was defective and on the occasion of the opening ceremonies, a large part of a wall was blown out through a short-circuit, right in the presence of old Emperor William I.** Germany refused to pay for the plant and the company was about to endure a crippling financial loss. As it stood, the power plant was useless.

Because of my position in the company, my many recent successes, and my skill with speaking German, I was asked to help fix this problem. I was not only tasked with going to the power plant to fix the problem by hand, but I was also meant to represent the company and win back the Germans' favor through persuasion. I was sent to Strasbourg to accomplish this in February of 1883.

The experiences I had in Strasbourg were not ones I would soon forget. Working in that power plant was hell, but the city itself was quite spectacular. A lot of the men who soon became famous throughout Europe lived in that city when I was visiting. For many years later, I would share stories about my life there and tell people, **"There were bacteria of greatness in that old town. Other's caught the disease, but I escaped!"**

Most of my time was not spent enjoying the nightlife. Working on that blasted power plant kept me busy and exhausted at all hours. I would often halt my work at the plant in order for the German government officials to summon me to their conferences, where I would ensure them of my productivity. When I finally made enormous progress and had practically replaced every wire in the building, I began to build an entirely new type of motor to generate power for the plant. It was the motor I had been dreaming of since my college years and the one that I finally designed that day at the park in Budapest. It was my motor of alternating currents.

I snuck out to a small tool shed across the railroad line from the power plant. I had brought some items from Paris for the project, and everything else I needed was located on-site. It took me until the end of August to finish working on the power plant, but I successfully built, by hand, the first motor of alternating currents in that shed. When it was all over, I had successfully taken the worst excuse for a power plant and transformed it into the most advanced facility in the world. A year after my vision in Budapest, I had finally built what I saw possible. This was the first induction motor ever built.

The job of rebuilding the plant had been a very tedious operation, but once it was finished I could finally enjoy some leisure in the beautiful city of Strasbourg. I was given special privilege and access to this gorgeous place, because my work had done the mayor a great favor in relieving his worst anxieties. He introduced me to the city's businessmen and other notable citizens, and parties and dinners abounded across the town.

It was a marvelous time in my life. The mayor and I chatted endlessly and I told him of many of my new inventions and ideas. He promised me that he would relay these ideas to some of the city's financial elite for potential business opportunities. I was quite excited by the prospects, but I was let down when nothing came of it. The path towards success is littered with disappointments.

The mayor wanted to show me his gratitude, still, and gave me a lovely gift. In his possession were crates full of bottles of St. Estephe dated 1801. He had buried an ample supply of the wine in 1870 during the German invasion of France. It was fine wine, and although I would have preferred money and business partnerships at the time, it was very much appreciated and did not go to waste. Seeing this treasure trove of fine wine given to me was a clear sign that bigger things were soon to come. The mayor's hospitality was a gift I could never repay.

My new friend, the mayor, advised that I would find financial backing for my new motor in Paris and pushed me to go back to the city as soon as I could. **This I was anxious to do, but my work and negotiations were protracted, owing to all sorts of petty obstacles I**

**encountered, so that at times the situation seemed hopeless.** Working with the Germans there in Strasbourg had been a complete nightmare. It was total and constant frustration inside the corporate structure of that power plant.

We rewired the entire facility, bit by bit. During one instance there was an additional lighting fixture that was being added to a hallway. I selected the best location for the light to be placed and gave my instruction to the mechanic beneath me to have it installed and to lay down the copper wiring through the walls. I returned to my work, and after an hour or so he came back to report. He said that no further action could be done without the approval of the team engineer, and so I put down my tools and we left together to find this engineer. It was a waste of time and I was very much annoyed, but there was no other choice.

The engineer squabbled for a while and reasoned against my instructions, but finally concluded that the lighting fixture should be installed a mere two inches from the point I had chosen. The mechanic then went back to his work installing the light in that hallway. Then, that engineer anxiously returned to say that his supervising inspector must be given notice of our action. That inspector arrived and examined the situation. He and the other engineer argued, and he concluded that the light ought to be moved two inches to the left, the exact place I had selected the day before!

My worries with this situation were not over yet. Another hour passed. The supervising inspector returned and anxiously explained that he had decided to notify the chief inspector above him, and that progress must again come to a halt until we had further approval. They could not have been more inefficient.

It was about three days before the chief inspector had the time to come and judge the case. He must have been busy, for apparently he had to inspect every sneeze the workers made. Once he arrived, the engineer, supervising inspector, lead inspector, and myself all argued for two hours and finally the chief inspector asserted that the light be moved back two more inches again. I didn't care one bit. I was beyond pleased that this business was over and I could get along with larger matters.

Alas, this was still not the case! Later, the chief inspector returned to me to say, "The government appointed councilor to oversee this operation is explicit in his demand that you must not have any lighting fixtures placed without his expressed authorization." Furthermore, he told me, this high ranking official was now scheduled to make a formal appearance to the power plant because of our insubordination.

For his visit, we had to spend a half day cleaning. They wanted not only the saw dust swept, but all the metals polished as well. The level of cleanliness and presentation they required was a bit much for a non-functioning plant under construction, in my opinion, but this was apparently a very important government official.

When the man arrived, he came with a group of advisors and assistants. What followed was an observance of protocol in which they all stood in a line and met with one another individually. There was almost no discussion of the business at hand, and everyone was concerned with exchanging formal pleasantries. **After two hours of deliberation, he suddenly exclaimed, "I must be going!" and pointing to a place on the ceiling, he ordered me to put the lamp there. It was the exact spot which I had originally chosen!**

I spent the year with many headaches of this sort. We finished the project in the spring of the following year, and the German government approved the plant. Strasbourg is a beautiful town, but I was at my wits end after the ordeal. I was excited to get back to Paris for several reasons. For one, I had been promised a hefty bonus in the event that I could get the power plant up and running again and accepted by the Germans. I was also owed another bonus for improving the generators in Paris just before being called away. All things considered, I had a large amount of money waiting for me in Paris.

To receive my bonus, I spoke to the three top directors of the company individually. The first gentleman told me that I must speak with the second. The second told me to speak to the third. Alas, the third was adamant in telling me that no one other than the first man had the authority to bestow the funds I was owed. After chasing this circle of administrators for several rounds, **it dawned upon me that my reward was a castle in Spain.** Which is to say, I received no bonus for my hard work. It was the first, but not the last time I would be cheated for helping one of Edison's companies.

All the time, I was still hopelessly trying to raise funding to start my own company with my alternating current generator, and without an ounce of success. My job had kept me far too busy to pursue my own business ventures. Soon after returning to Paris, Mr. Charles Bachelor offered me a chance to go to America to continue to work for Edison's primary company there to help repair many of his generators, with the possibility of helping design new ones. I leapt at the opportunity. I would have been a fool not to take the chance to continue my travels across the world, and so **I determined to try my fortunes in the land of the golden promise.**

I sold most of my belongings, which didn't amount to much, and soon enough found myself waiting at the train station to begin my journey to this faraway place. The train locomotive roared into the station, and I looked up to discover that my luggage had been stolen!

I had no ticket, no money, nothing but the books in my hand. I had only moments to decide what to do. I thought briefly that perhaps I should stay in Paris. It seemed unlikely that I could show up to the New World with nothing but the clothes on my back and be able to get far. But it seemed like my life was not moving forward in Paris, and I did have a job waiting for me in the United States. I managed to convince the ticket usher that I was genuinely owed access to the train, and as the train was departing he allowed me to jump aboard.

I almost never left Europe because of this thief, yet fate decided that this would not be the case for me. Without much other than a few notebooks in my hand, I made my way from the train, then to the passenger vessel, and finally to America. **Later, when I had absorbed some of the practical American sense, I shivered at the recollection and marveled at my former folly.**

Mister Bachelor had arranged for me to meet Thomas Edison, and a few days after landing in New York I formally met the great man. He had always been someone I admired and **I was amazed at this wonderful man who, without early advantages and scientific training, had accomplished so much.** There I was, meeting a great idol of mine.

I had spent my life reading every book I could get my hands on and learning everything I could from scientific works like Newton's *Principia* to the literary works of Charles de Kock. I had obsessed with learning everything I could about the natural world and it had all payed off when I quickly won the respect of Edison. I was overjoyed to be working directly for him.

One of Edison's major projects was for a commercial steam boat by the name of the S.S. Oregon. For a while, no other passenger ship could match the top speed of the Oregon. It was also the first passenger ship to have electrical lighting. Needless to say, the ship was a popular mode of transportation.

The ship had two large electrical generators to power the lighting and both of them were busted. The ship sat idle, stalled at the seaport for electrical renovations. It was impossible to take the generators outside of the ship—because the ship had been built around them, trapping the large machines inside. This made these generators particularly hard to manage and repair. **The predicament was a serious one and Edison was much annoyed.**

After my first meeting with Edison in the United States, he asked me to help him repair the S.S. Oregon to its full functionality. I insisted it would be done. That night, I gathered my tools and boarded the massive boat, and I worked there until just before sunrise. It was a tricky task.

Once I laid eyes upon the machines, I was able to see for myself how truly ruined they were. Countless components were broken and the wiring short circuited. I knew exactly what to do; I gave instructions to the crew and began to get my own hands dirty. It was a sorry sight, but I had seen worse in Germany. Bureaucracy would not stall me this time.

Early the next morning, I had left the Oregon and was walking back to the shop. As I was crossing Fifth Avenue, I encountered Edison with his crew—it was Charles Bachelor and the other gentleman that made up the usual crowd that accompanied Edison. It was five o'clock in the morning, and they were all leaving their office from a hard night of work.

**"Here is our Parisian running around at night,"** [Edison said.] **When I told him that I was coming from the Oregon and had repaired both machines, he looked at me in silence and walked away without another word. But when he had gone some distance, I heard him remark, "Bachelor, this is a good man."** After that, I had earned the respect of Edison and was granted the liberty to pursue my work in his company without anyone looking over my shoulders.

I arrived to fulfill my duties every morning at 10:30 a.m. and would work until 5:00 a.m. the following day. I did this for just shy of a year and took no personal days or weekends to rest. The inventor often said to me, **"I have had many hard working assistants, but you take the cake."**

It was not time wasted, because I gained a practical insider's view of the workings of a company like Edison's. However, I did not feel so lucky nearing the end of my term working for the man. The inventor I had admired for so long had taken advantage of me. This had become all too clear in an instant, and I decided that was the last day I would ever work for him again.

Edison had told me he would pay me a sum of $50,000[4] if I reconstructed every machine his company possessed, using a significantly better design. Thus, for almost a full year, I poured my sweat on a daily basis to accomplish this task with the promise that I would be a rich man for it. **I designed twenty-four different types of standard machines with short cores and uniform pattern, which replaced the old ones. On completion of this task, it turned out to be a practical joke.**

---

[4] Well over a million dollars in today's money.

Edison had never intended to pay me a cent more than my meager wages of eighteen dollars a week. I had asked for a raise to twenty-five dollars a week several times and was denied even that. But this was the final straw. The moment Thomas Edison told me I was a fool to take him seriously at his offer to pay me for services rendered, I decided I would not be his fool for a minute longer. I walked right out of his office and left him forever.

**Immediately thereafter, some people approached me with the proposal of forming an arc light company under my name, to which I agreed.** Arc lights, if you are not familiar, are very bright lights used for flood lighting, including for lighthouses. At the time, arc lighting was far from perfect, but my new company made drastic improvements and my design became the new standard in arc lighting.

I should have been happy about this accomplishment, but at the time I was very upset because of my lack of control over the company. When these men had first approached me to create a business, I was very excited to finally have the opportunity to produce my new motor on a large scale, but when I spoke about the prospect, they said flatly,

**"No, we want the arc lamp. We don't care for this alternating current of yours."**

It was a long time before the arc lights improved my lot in life. The two years that followed after I had walked out on Edison were some of the most difficult of my life. Thankfully, through hard work, I eventually turned my luck around. **There were many days when [I] did not know where my next meal was coming from, but I was never afraid to work. I went to where some men were digging a ditch, [and] said I wanted to work. The boss looked at my good clothes and white hands and he laughed to the others, but he said, "All right. Spit on your hands. Get in the ditch." I worked harder than anybody. At the end of the day, I had two dollars.**

My time was split between designing arc lights, meeting with business associates, and digging ditches for less money than Edison had been paying me. By the next year, in 1886, my method for producing arc lighting was finally executed and embraced for use in factories. I was an instant success, at least in theoretical terms.

In truth, I came out of the ordeal with **no other possession than a beautifully engraved certificate of stock of hypothetical value.**

I continued to struggle for survival, living a double life as both a professional and a common worker. I would throw on a suit and clean my appearance when I was needed for a board meeting, sometimes immediately after digging ditches. The first signs of higher success came in April of the following year when the Tesla Electric Company was formally constructed, complete with an office, my personal laboratory, and other amenities. I wasted no time in making more of the induction motors I sought to make widespread, and began their creation as soon as I had access to my laboratory.

The good men who had helped me launch my company weren't interested in the idea, but I would make it happen with or without them. **The motors I built there were exactly as I had imaged them. I made no attempts to improve the design, but merely reproduced the pictures as they appeared to my vision, and [their] operation was always as I expected.**

It took almost a year, but in 1888 I had found a perfect partner for the machine in a wonderful man named George Westinghouse. The Westinghouse Company deployed the power stations, and the Tesla Electric Company supplied the motors inside them. Our two companies would work in harmony for a decade to follow. With Westinghouse, I was now working as a direct competitor to Edison for both lighting and electrical power.

I left New York for a trip to Pittsburgh to begin our partnership. There, I met with the Westinghouse board of directors and toured their factories. The electrical system that had been adopted at Westinghouse was based on high frequency currents, but my motor was based on a system of my own creation that was designed at low currents. The Westinghouse people were not willing to change their method to adapt for a system of low currents, and so it was decided that I would make alterations to my motor for their purposes.

My presence in Pennsylvania was no longer needed towards the end of 1889. I left the smoky city full of factories and returned to New York to immediately begin work to revise my machine to suit Westinghouse's plan. I was moving up in the world quickly, and now had a new laboratory on Grand Street.

Using high frequencies seemed impractical to me, but it would be a massive and expensive overhaul for Westinghouse to do otherwise, so I happily submitted to do my part. **The problems of construction in this** unexplored field were novel and quite peculiar, and I encountered many difficulties.

My biggest obstacle for creating an alternating current generator designed for high-frequency electrical currents was the difficulty in maintaining a machine that operated with a consistent speed. For my initial attempts, the generator would pulse erratically when creating power. It would always work fine initially, but rapidly break down. I eventually devised a high-frequency generator with the necessary equal distribution, resulting in a low, unabating hum that was music to my ears. I then made a second, and much greater discovery completely by accident.

It appeared that I would need to invent a very small device to make this high-frequency machine a possibility. There needed to be a way to facilitate electrical oscillations within a much smaller generator. The device would need to distribute the oscillations internally and keep them consistent in relation to one another so as not to overheat. **In 1856, Lord Kelvin had exposed the theory of the condenser discharge, but [up to this point] no practical application of that important knowledge was made.**

Kelvin's discovery often gave me grand ideas to think about, but nothing concrete until this instance. As I was working to rebuild my motor for Westinghouse, it was Kelvin's theory that gave me yet another eureka moment. It was suddenly clear to me that I could use this concept to construct a small induction device which could render a working AC motor of high-frequency currents.

I had so much success with creating the device, that just over a year later I was comfortable sharing my work during my 1891 lecture at the American Institution of Electrical Engineers. It was there I first displayed to an audience my creation of **a coil giving sparks of five inches.**

**Since my early announcement of the invention, it has come into universal use and wrought a revolution in many departments, but a still greater future awaits it. When in 1900, I obtained powerful discharges of 1,000 feet and flashed a [wireless] current around the globe [from my laboratory in Colorado], I was reminded of the first tiny spark I observed in my Grand Street laboratory and was**

thrilled by sensations akin to those I felt when I discovered the rotating magnetic field[5].

---

[5] The rotating magnetic field is another way of describing an alternating current motor, also known as an induction motor.

# PART FIVE

As I sit here and recount these moments from long ago, I'm coming to realize how events so small that they appeared meaningless have actually largely impacted my life. I shall tell you one instance from my boyhood that will provide a marvelous example. Other young boys and I made a difficult hike far upward on a snowy mountain.

We left deep footprints as our boots compacted the snow on our journey. It was the harsh of winter, but the south wind had brought with it a warm breeze for the week, making prime conditions for our mountain expedition. On reaching a high cliff, we simply stopped and admired the breathtaking view of the surrounding lands from up high.

It was not long before that admiration turned into boyhood games. One of my companions threw a ball of snow into the air ahead of us and we all watched as the ball fell down below and slowly disappeared out of sight. Right then, another one of my fair friends took a larger ball of snow, and instead, gently pushed it down the mountain. The ball rolled and picked up some small amounts of snow as it went, and thereby gradually grew larger as it went further below.

We each began to follow his example, and watched as the balls became bigger as they rolled down the mountain. Sometimes one would hit a rock and shatter into dust. Otherwise, the balls would eventually get so far down the mountain that we would lose sight of their movement completely. We had such a fun time of this, but then one ball did something different. It accumulated so much snow that it became the size of a small building, and the ground shook as it collided into the valley below.

I was hypnotized. We looked at one another in fear and amazement at what we had just done. Hopefully, there was no one else out in the snow below us, we all thought. The avalanche surely could have killed someone, but that amazing moment stuck in my mind. The sight had left me with an unquenchable need to know more.

How could something so tiny quickly become so gigantic? I watched the scene play out in my head again and again many times over the following weeks. It woke a curiosity within me that I followed for the rest of my life.

From that point onward, I have been obsessed with the idea of magnification. A decade later, I had become a formal student in the science of electricity. At the time, the field was still an experimental study. My obsession for magnification went hand in hand with my curiosity of this mysterious force called electricity. I cannot say for certain, but had I not seen that avalanche in my boyhood, I may not have become the man known as Nikola Tesla. **I might not have followed up the little spark I obtained with my coil and never developed my best invention.**

My Tesla coil was a major shift in the way we human beings can use electricity[6]. There have been many people who have suggested that I have done almost nothing to change the world, apart for my induction motor. Many of these men are even intelligent, but it is obvious to me that they are unable to clearly see the big picture. It is my pleasure to explain to

---

[6] The Tesla coil was an early form of a transformer.

you just how very wrong these critics of mine have been.

I assure you, my deeds will radically transform the future for hundreds of years to come. I will expand upon how and why, but first I shall give you an idea of how slowly society accepts change. The bladeless turbine I invented is a marvelous example of this. You would think that if a better form of a device was presented it would be immediately embraced, but that is simply not the case when you are dealing with things on an industrial scale. Billions of dollars have been spent on the existing turbines in this country. Replacing them with better turbines is not something the business owners are the least bit concerned with doing, and in fact, it would be to their detriment.

Under a better system, of course, this would not be the case. But in the current environment, advancements must be made very slowly. The business owners are the only ones in the position to make the changes, and optimal performance is logically sacrificed for practicality. Why, just a few days ago I experienced a disappointing conversation on this subject when I bumped into my former assistant, Charles F. Scott.

Charles is a good friend of mine who is currently teaching electrical engineering at Yale. I had not seen him for a long time and was glad to have an opportunity for a little chat at my office. Our conversation, naturally enough, drifted on my turbine and I became heated to a high degree. "Scott," I exclaimed, carried away by the vision of a glorious future, "My turbine will scrap all the heat engines in the world[!]" Scott stroked his chin and looked away thoughtfully. "That will make quite a pile of scrap," he said. Then, he just walked right out of the room without so much as saying goodbye.

My turbine and several other of my inventions are solid improvements, but they are nothing but advancements on already established models. Improvements for the existing ideas are going to happen with or without my help. Now, again, I address my critics. The true mark of an inventor is to bring entirely *new* ideas into the world. My device, the magnifying transmitter, is one such invention.

If my memory serves me right, it was in November 1890, that I performed a laboratory experiment which was one of the most extraordinary and spectacular ever recorded in the annals of science. I was rebuilding my induction motor to function at high electrical currents for the purposes of the Westinghouse Electric Company. I decided to play around with those high frequency currents. It seemed to me that I could create an invisible electrical field within the room and so I decided to find a way to test this.

I crafted a glass lightbulb and sat it on the table. Unlike the kind of bulb you might use on a regular basis, this one had no electrode, and was not made to be plugged into a wall socket. I placed it near an induction motor I'd been toying with and fired up the machine. This generated an electrical field. As soon as the motor took an appreciable speed, I stepped back, and watched the lightbulb as it sat on the table, now pulsing with a powerful glow. In that moment, it dawned on me that with my magnifying transmitter, I had made wires obsolete.

That was 29 years ago. You see, my turbines may never catch on in the industrial sector. When the time comes to update the factories and buildings with new equipment, someone else will have already come along to create a much better turbine. But this magnifying transmitter of mine, and the ability to create wireless energy straight from the source into any electrical device will one day become the standard of electrical use. There will be no need for wires. You will simply flip a switch and receive power to your device through the air from a transmitter. It might take a long time for this to happen, but one day it is inevitable.

I felt a great excitement when I discovered this invention, but not near the amount as when I had finally accomplished the construction of my induction motor. It is strange, but we feel less excitement as we grow older. This discovery was much more important than my motor, and yet I felt only a fraction of the excitement when I first saw my creation come to life. When I showed my wireless lightbulbs to the public for the first time, I must say, those were some of the widest eyes I have ever seen.

After the presentation, I began to receive a flood of letters from all over the world. So many institutions wanted my attention to give me honors or request to induct me into their societies. Everyone wanted to see and be associated with Nikola Tesla. It was such an honor, but I just wanted to be left alone to finish the work.

In 1892 the offers became so good, I happily stalled my work and left for Europe. I spoke in London before the Institution of Electrical Engineers. I told them how I discovered my Tesla coil and my magnifying transmitter, and I showed them my wireless lightbulbs to explain a future without wires or batteries. I was thrilled to share my work and spent hours at these lectures, sharing as many of my discoveries as I could. For a bit of fun, I even showed them how high voltage electricity could pass through a human body without harm, if you know what you are doing.

First, I would produce a large bolt of electricity to show as an example. Then I would continue my lecture, **"But through calculation and reason, I concluded that such currents ought not to be dangerous to life any more than the vibrations of light are dangerous."** I would say this exact phrase before moving my hand upward into the air and towards the bolt of electricity. **"A spark passes through my hands, and may puncture the skin, and sometimes I receive an occasional burn, but that is all; and even this can be avoided if I hold a conductor of suitable size in my hand and then take hold of the current."**

Performing these lectures was a humbling experience, and what followed was one of the best moments of my life. I was scheduled to arrive in Paris the next day to prepare my next lecture in French, but I was given temptation to stay in London. **Sir James Dewar[7] insisted on my appearing before the Royal Institution.** I made it clear that I was leaving for Paris, but his Scottish charm swayed me as he made his demands. **He pushed me into a chair and poured out half a glass of a wonderful brown fluid which sparkled in all sorts of iridescent colors and tasted like nectar.**

"Now," said he, "you are sitting in Faraday's chair and you are enjoying whiskey he used to drink." I had mostly lost my taste for liquors by that age, but this was all too convincing. After drinking the glass, I decided that Paris would have to wait. The following night, I repeated my lecture at the Royal Institution at his persuasion. Lord Rayleigh spoke at the close of my presentation, and I had never felt so honored to be recognized by some of the greatest living men on Earth.

After London and Paris, I couldn't get a moment's rest. So many people wanted to talk to me. I escaped Paris to visit home and see my family, but my mind was very anxious from dealing with so many people. I had excited

---

[7] Sir James Dewar invented the original vacuum flask, now most commonly known as a Thermos.

myself too much, and my body suffered another peculiar breakdown. Once again, I was in complete agony and at the mercy of my own body.

I recovered from my illness fairly quickly this time and set my sights on continuing my work and research in America. **Up to that time, I never realized that I possessed any particular gift of discovery, but Lord Rayleigh, whom I always considered as an ideal man of science, had said so and if that was the case, I felt that I should concentrate on some big idea.**

I had brought so many new inventions into existence. I was already rapidly changing the ways in which human beings lived, but I wanted to do something even bigger. I wanted to think of one big idea that would overshadow my already enormous contributions. I didn't know where to begin, and so I returned to the teachings of the Bible.

My mother had always taught me that inner strength comes from God and the traditions described within the Bible, and the time spent with my family after giving my lectures reinforced these values for me. I decided I would stay in Europe for the next few months to return to a study of the Scriptures. Many times in my life, I have paused my work to do the very same. Nearing the end of those months, my next big idea finally emerged.

I went hiking alone in the mountainside to read and reflect in peace. A storm of heavy winds and rain quickly emerged just moments after the sky gave a brief performance of lightning. The short moments when the sky was covered in dark clouds before the rain had begun to fall were what caught my curiosity.

The more I thought about it, the lightning seemed to have been provoking the rain and the wind into the disturbance that I witnessed. This is surely not the case for every storm, but the lightning seemed to initiate the other harsh weather conditions in this particular event, once the dark clouds had been set in place. Seeing this so closely gave me another great epiphany.

It would be quite possible to have some control in creating weather conditions. The sun's heat transfers groundwater into vapor, moving it high into the air. Changes in atmosphere cause the water vapor to form back into a liquid and fall. Strong winds can bring cold and warm fronts from neighboring places. Warm air and cool air colliding together can create storms.

**[This would be a] stupendous possibility of achievement.** Each of these instances simply requires a specific type of energy to be applied to a precise location. There's no reason human beings cannot supply the energy for these changes. Heat created by a machine could transform water into vapor instead of the sun, for example. There are conceivable ways of creating wind, just as well.

**If we could produce electric effects of the required quality, this whole planet and the conditions of existence on it could be transformed. The sun raises the water of the oceans and winds drive it to distant regions where it remains in a state of most delicate balance. If it were in our power to upset it when and wherever desired, this mighty life sustaining stream could be at will controlled. We could irrigate arid deserts, create lakes and rivers, and provide motive power in unlimited amounts.**

Energy production will increase significantly once human beings can do this. As we collect energy from the sun to convert into electricity, so begins the process. The more energy we are able to produce in the beginning of each of these cycles, the more energy we will then collect in return. Additionally, if we can control the wind, we will collect more wind energy.

Soon after my hike, I decided that my retreat to Europe was at its end. I would travel back to my home in the United States and focus on the big idea I had finally found. To control the weather, I would need three things. I would need the ability to produce large amounts of heat, wind, and lighting on command. Heat and wind seemed to me by far the easiest to create. I began working at once to produce lightning bolts equal to those found in nature.

Very soon at my lab on Fifth Avenue in New York, my **work was begun, which was to me all the more attractive, because a means of the same kind was necessary for the successful transmission of energy without wires.** Just as I was beginning my experiments, I came across problems in the work that deeply puzzled me. They seemed impossible to solve. I again returned to my Bible, and the answer came to me as I was reading the book of Revelation.

**The first gratifying result was obtained in the spring of the succeeding year, when I reached a tension of about 100,000,000 volts—one hundred million volts— with my**

**conical coil.** I did not know the voltage of a bolt of lightning in nature, but I supposed that it would be close to this. My work towards voltage in even greater numbers resumed, until March of 1895. My laboratory was the entire fourth floor of a building at 33 South Fifth Avenue, and one day it was all suddenly gone in a mysterious fire that collapsed the whole building[8].

**This calamity set me back in many ways, and most of that year had to be devoted to planning and reconstruction.** I lost all of my research equipment and many unique items of my own creation in that fire. My old friend, Thomas Edison, was gracious enough to let me use his lab in New Jersey for a while. It was especially nice of him, considering he was telling the newspapers that my AC electric power was dangerous, and that people should only rely on his direct current electricity.

The joke was soon on Edison. He had applied to engineer and construct the first large-scale hydroelectric power plant at Niagara Falls. My partner, Mr. Westinghouse, and I had submitted our own designs as well. Lord Kelvin himself was appointed as the commissioner to oversee this project, and he chose

---

[8] A very mysterious fire indeed…

my designs of alternating current to build the plant. We won the contract.

The fire that destroyed my lab couldn't have come at a worse time[9]. Months later, my business dealings were finished, and I could finally return to the big ideas I was developing towards new applications of electricity. I replaced my old lab with a shining new laboratory on Houston Street, and soon I had a brand new invention. It was a totally new type of transmitter.

Much like the one used in my previous laboratory, before the fire, this device could create lightning of one hundred million volts. It was obvious that I could increase this voltage with a larger device, but for safety reasons I decided on creating a more sleek and smaller design. I was very happy with the progress, but I needed a place where I could make very large bolts of lightning without risks of fire. I needed to leave the city.

**In order to advance further along this line, I had to go into the open, and in the spring of**

---

[9] The eyewitness to this fire worked as the night watchman for the building, and he was the only person working there at the time of the fire. He claimed the fire began from the basement and climbed upward. Tesla's lab only occupied the 4th floor, suggesting that the fire did not originate from his lab.

1899, having completed preparations for the erection of a wireless plant, I went to Colorado where I remained for more than one year. In Colorado, I fine-tuned my ideas concerning these machines. I was able to build a transformer that could produce a steady electric flow of virtually any amount of high voltages. The device could provide continuous power for all of society.

I will be quite explicit on the subject of my magnifying transformer. Its primary purpose is as a resonant transformer, which is simply a device able to create very high voltages at very high frequencies. The particulars of my device involve the use of a very large ring. This ring functions to contain many small panels that are conductively isolated to decrease the density of electrical energy passing through each panel across the surface of the ring. The result is a capacitor capable of tapping into the resonance of the upper atmosphere in order to collect electricity.

The maximum electric tension is merely dependent on the curvature of the surfaces on which the charged elements are situated and the area of the latter. Judging from my past experience, there is no limit to the possible voltage developed; any amount is

**practicable.** The amperage achieved is not so seemingly infinite but will reach into the thousands. I can produce electricity for the entire world, and without the use of diesel fuels. **Those who are interested will find some information in regard to the experiments I conducted there in my article, "The Problem of Increasing Human Energy," in the Century Magazine of June 1900.**

My magnifying transformer is the key piece of machinery needed for my great plan. With it, a power plant of relatively small size could provide power to an entire region. **Theoretically, a terminal of less than 90 feet in diameter is sufficient to develop [the necessary] electromotive force. It need not be larger than 30 feet in diameter. Such a circuit may then be excited with impulses of any kind, even of low frequency, and it will yield continuous oscillations like those of an alternator.**

With these dimensions, the transformer **is accurately proportioned to fit the globe and its electrical constants and properties, by virtue of which design it becomes highly efficient and effective in the wireless transmission of energy.** There is virtually nothing to dampen the wireless signal, and so **distance is then absolutely eliminated. It is even possible to** make the actions increase with the distance from the plant, according to an exact mathematical law.

I have already built a station of this description, and it was operating perfectly in providing the wireless transmission of power. It can be done, and although I have succeeded once, I quickly lost possession of the property upon which the power station was built. The issue was a lack of funds. J.P. Morgan had supplied the $150,000 to purchase the property, but later wanted his money back. I pleaded with him that this would benefit both him and all of the world greatly, but failed to convince him of this obvious truth.

I have shared with you my life, and now we have come to the point at which I can finally tell you about my current project. It is always difficult to do the impossible, but I have done it once before. Every scientist with a reputation to protect would have told you that the invention of an alternating current motor was impossible before I invented it. Just as well, no one believes that my current areas of research are to be taken seriously. Yet, I have already built it and seen it perform brilliantly with my own eyes. I created a wireless power station at Long Island, New York.

The invention of a wireless power station is only but a single part of many that are included within my **world system of wireless transmission.** My world system will revolutionize the way people communicate. It will give the common man constant luxury in many ways. When I left Colorado to come back home to New York City in the year of 1900, I began at once to build my first tower.

I made a public statement soon after, to announce the following details about the invention. **The world system has resulted from a combination of several original discoveries made by the inventor in the course of long continued research and experimentation. It makes possible not only the instantaneous and precise wireless transmission of any kind of signals, messages or characters, to all parts of the world, but also the interconnection of the existing telegraph, telephone, and other signal stations without any change in their present equipment. By its means, for instance, a telephone subscriber here may call up and talk to any other subscriber on Earth.**

**An inexpensive receiver, not bigger than a watch, will enable him to listen anywhere, on land or sea, to a speech delivered or music playing in some other place, however distant.**

The technology will come to have endless uses, some that may be beyond my imagination. These are only a few examples I can offer to suggest what the system will be able to do, but people will continue to find more uses for it. It will be a **great scientific advance** that makes all communication instant, no matter the distance.

My invention uses the Earth itself as a conductor and can send transmissions and power wirelessly in the same way that has been done with the use of long-distance power cables. Any device that requires the use of wires for an electric charge will never again need access to a wire for power. The distance from the power station and any given device is almost irrelevant. **Thus, not only will entirely new fields for commercial exploitation be opened up by this ideal method of transmission, but the old ones vastly extended. The world system is based on the application of the following import and inventions and discoveries—**

1. **The Tesla Transformer: This apparatus is in the production of electrical vibrations as revolutionary as gunpowder was in warfare. Currents many times stronger than any ever generated in the usual ways**

and sparks over one hundred feet long, have been produced by the inventor with an instrument of this kind.

2. The Magnifying Transmitter: This is [my] best invention, a peculiar transformer specially adapted to excite the Earth, which is in the transmission of electrical energy what the telescope is in astronomical observation. By the use of this marvelous device, [I have] already set up electrical movements of greater intensity than those of lightning and passed a current, sufficient to light more than two hundred incandescent lamps, around the Earth.

3. The Tesla Wireless System: This system comprises a number of improvements and is the only means known for transmitting, economically, electrical energy to a distance without wires. Careful test and measurements in connection with an experimental station of great activity, erected by the inventor in Colorado, have demonstrated that power in any desired amount can be conveyed, clear across the globe if necessary, with a[n energy] loss not exceeding a few percent.

4.  The Art of Individualization: This invention of Tesla is to primitive tuning, what refined language is to unarticulated expression. It makes possible the transmission of signals or messages absolutely secret and exclusive both in the active and passive aspect, that is, non-interfering as well as non-interferable. Each signal is like an individual of unmistakable identity and there is virtually no limit to the number of stations or instruments which can be simultaneously operated without the slightest mutual disturbance.

5.  The Terrestrial Stationary Waves: This wonderful discovery, popularly explained, means that the Earth is responsive to electrical vibrations of definite pitch, just as a tuning fork to certain waves of sound. These particular electrical vibrations, capable of powerfully exciting the globe, lend themselves to innumerable uses of great importance commercially and in many other respects. The first world system can be put into operation in nine months. With this power plant, it will be practicable to attain electrical activities up to ten million horsepower, and it is designed to serve for as many technical

achievements as are possible without due expense. Among these are the following:

- The world system will connect the already existing telephone offices that operate throughout the world.

- The world system allows for private messages to be sent. It will not be possible for anyone other than the intended receiver to spy on the transmission. This will increase national security.

- Personal letters will be sent wirelessly and in an instant around the world using the world system. The world system will distribute the newspapers as well as news radio. Music will be distributed via the world system.

- The world system will synchronize the stock tickers of the world. Just as well, the clocks will be synchronized. Time will be kept more accurately and without any need for regular adjustment of the instruments.

- Checks will be sent via the world system.

- The world system will replace the compass. Ships at sea will have a wireless navigation system that will show them their precise location. Just as well, any of the functions listed here will work both on land and sea.

- Photographs will be sent as well from one place to another in an instant. Transcripts, works of art, and records of any kind will be sent via the world system.

There are other uses for my world system that will dwarf the functions that I have listed. I am not yet comfortable revealing the full uses of my inventions, but I will announce the rest of them in the future. First, I must secure a massive amount of funding.

The tower I once built on Long Island was 187 feet tall and was capable of providing wireless power to the surrounding region. Taking a meager 200-300 kilowatts, the station could magnify that energy to create enough electricity to power all of New York. That station was taken away from me and destroyed two years ago.

All of my time and energy is now devoted to building a new one. I will do it as soon as I am able. **My project was retarded by the laws of nature. The world was not prepared for it. It was too far ahead of time, but the same laws will prevail in the end and make it a triumphal success.**

**On this occasion, I would [like to] contradict the widely circulated report that the structure was demolished by the [United States] government.** I need not remind my readers that the Great War has only ended months ago. At the time, the government would have had much to gain from having this advanced technology. Strange rumors against my character have sprouted from nothing other than the fact that I am a foreigner, and during this hideous European war, fear has taken the best of people. Perhaps a common man does not know the name Nikola Tesla, and thereby becomes suspicious of my nationality and allegiance.

I would like to remind my readers that thirty years ago, I was granted the **honor of American citizenship.** While I keep some of my most valuable belongings such as my honorary degrees and gold medals in storage trunks, my prized citizenship documents are kept in a locked safe. This is the only home I have left, and I wish the best for this nation.

I have never been suspected of treasonous efforts, and any of my dealings with the authorities have been pleasant and with mutual honor. I have explained to everyone in the government I have met with the idea that our military could track our own submarines during wartime with my inventions. Critical missions would be easily won with the tools I have created.

I tell every official that I am at the service of this country. America is my home. The land of my birth is dear to me and has been devastated by generations of war. It is my duty to offer my assistance in national defense, so that the horrors of war will never touch the United States of America. A free society must not be threatened, because peace is so absolutely rare. Science, art, and culture all flourish when each individual lives with freedom from oppression.

My passion on this subject is such that I have even given pause to my own business pursuits in order to do a minor study on the art of war. **My plant, services, and all my improvements have always been at the disposal of the officials and ever since the outbreak of the European conflict, I have been working at a sacrifice on several inventions of mine relating to aerial navigation, ship propulsion and wireless transmission, which are of the greatest importance to the country.** I would freely offer my talents to assist in the invention and production of wartime technologies, and without any thought of financial gain. May this country never suffer the same devastation as my Serbian people, and may God bless America.

Secondly, I would like to address rumors concerning myself and J. P. Morgan. Morgan is an honorable man. I very much respect his massive influence that has advanced our society. He helped me in my career many times, because he is a man that always tries to do good. He has helped many rising entrepreneurs. He does it because he recognizes talent and good will. I am thankful for all the assistance he has given me.

He did not wish to further fund my career in the invention of a world system. I do not blame him. Mr. Morgan did what any businessman would have done. It is unfortunate, but my idea is about more than making profits. I want to give free power to all people. I want to give it in unlimited amounts.

# PART SIX

I must warn you. If you believe these technologies are not possible, you will certainly not believe what I am going to tell you about the future. While the key to my world system is my invention, the magnifying transmitter, I think the principle idea of my next invention comes from a place of deep observation of myself and the human spirit. I have created the notion of automation and the creation of intelligences from artificial life.

It is an idea that I have been cultivating for many decades now. I have struggled to make these concepts a reality, but I have successfully taken the largest first steps. I have put forth the building blocks that will bring about countless technological innovations. These technologies will grow stronger over time and continue to do so long after I am gone. The basic principles are set in place, and it is inevitable that one day all of our work will be done by machines. A time will come soon where gadgets will appear to have a mind of their own.

It was during that same period of building my tower on Long Island, when I was pushing myself to make advanced discoveries in this field of automation. Everything I have done before this point has been difficult to achieve, but this reduced my energy to the point of complete depletion. I fell into a deep slumber. When I am focused on an idea so intently, I chase it at the neglect of my own health.

I work by a specific style of focus. While the average person would think yearly vacations are essential, I have scarcely taken any throughout my career. As long as I have science to pursue, I am satisfied with working all hours of the day and night. I work to the absolute limits of my body, and eventually I am forced to rest. I may also incur a severe nervous breakdown if I extend myself beyond the brink.

When I reach this exhaustion, it happens the same way every time. My mind reaches its limit and throws me into a trance from which I very quickly fall asleep. I seem to always sleep for exactly 30 minutes before waking up, and always in a stupor. At that point, I have become so exhausted from my focus on one all-consuming idea that the mere notion of science makes me nauseous.

I am inevitably forced to leave the thoughts of my work and return to taking care of myself. Each time without fail, I am revitalized with pleasant thoughts about the world and my anxieties are relieved. After a period of rest, I am surprised at my ability to return to my difficult engineering problems and tackle them with ease.

On Long Island, I pushed myself to the brink and not only did I collapse from a lack of energy, but I suffered another breakdown of the senses. The strangest thing happened directly after I regained consciousness. I remembered all of my scientific knowledge and curiosity, but the personal memories of my life and past were gone. I could only remember my earliest childhood life. I temporarily lost all of my memories.

I somewhat continued my work in the laboratory, and I replayed these memories over and over. Each night, I recalled them again. I gradually regained more and more of my childhood. Trapped in my laboratory by fear, I tried to travel forward through these memories past my childhood to recover my full identity. I remembered only that my name was

Nikola, and I remembered my mother. Every evening as I was beginning to fall asleep, I would see her again. I tried to remember more of her.

**The image of my mother was always the principal figure in the spectacle that slowly unfolded.** She was the first thing that came to mind, because I wanted someone there to comfort me. I continued to work towards scientific discovery, but I still did not know my own identity. Each night after my work, I would see more visions of my mother. **A consuming desire to see her again gradually took possession of me.**

In this confused state, I continued my daily work with this growing need to see my mother again. I wanted to stop and flee the laboratory, and see her once more, but I did not have the faintest idea of how to navigate the outside world. I was frightened, and I didn't even remember how I came to be in this laboratory. I didn't realize for weeks that I was even in New York, but eventually, I ventured past the main entrance to find my mailbox. A small stack of letters affirmed my name and location.

I was stuck in this condition of struggling with my memories for several months. Finally,

I had recovered all of my memories up to the point of 1892. It was almost springtime, and I **saw myself at the Hotel de la Paix in Paris.** I saw myself there in my hotel room again, and I saw myself waking up from one of these same slumbers that come from overworking. This gave more clues into my life, and I remembered that I had been a rising scientist and remembered my friendship with the likes of Lord Kelvin and other great men. I now too remembered fading in and out of consciousness many times in the past.

As more of these memories appeared before me each night, each vision was as if I was really there in the past. I experienced these life events for the very first time again. It was very emotional to recount so many moments from my life in this way.

I was now brave enough to leave my laboratory, having recalled my full identity. I packed a suitcase to leave immediately to see my mother. I was overwhelmed with gratitude for my family, and filled with sudden regret for neglecting time with them for decades. Then, another memory appeared to me that truly broke my heart. While packing to leave, I experienced again the moment from my past when I was informed that my mother was dying.

The sudden guilt of living so far away from the rest of my family was unbearable. This guilt lingers within me to this day, but it is balanced by the pride I feel for my contributions to society. My life's work and my sacrifices have given me peace of mind.

I am still sharp, but in my age I have lost much of my edge. I'm in excellent condition, but I become tired much more easily these days. I don't have the will to put up with large groups of people, much less speak in front of them. Nor do I have access to the laboratory facilities I once possessed. I still tinker, but it may be true that my biggest feats of accomplishment are behind me. I left the spotlight long ago, and there are already whispers to decry me as an inventor altogether.

Nevertheless, it gives me tremendous peace to know that my creations will continue to give joy to the world after I am gone. In generations to come, my technologies will evolve to become so fantastically beneficial. Mechanical beings with intelligences similar to our own will serve all of our needs. They will never grow tired, because they will be powered wirelessly, and energy will be abundant in the future.

There might be ways to harvest massive amounts of energy from the splitting of an atom. I don't believe this is a reasonable approach. If this could be done to create energy, it could be used just as easily to make terrifying weapons. **If we were to release the energy of atoms or discover some other way of developing cheap and unlimited power [from the splitting of atoms], this accomplishment, instead of being a blessing, might bring disaster to mankind.**

**This is one of the reasons why I feel certain that of all my inventions, the magnifying transmitter will prove most important and valuable for future generations.** Using many of my ideas, which will be well preserved in writing for long after I am gone, there will be a nearly unlimited supply of energy. The electronic devices of the world will have instant and unlimited power transmitted to them from the surrounding air. There will be no reason to conserve energy, because it will be superabundant.

Wireless energy will provide power to the many machines that will do all of our labors. They will make life much easier, everything from gardening to construction. Cooking, factory work, laundry, and any menial human labor you can think of will be automated and made to be perfectly fast and easy.

I am prompted to this prediction, not so much by thoughts of the commercial and industrial revolution which it will surely bring about, but of the humanitarian consequences of many achievements it makes possible. We are confronted with portentous problems which cannot be solved just by providing for our material existence, however abundantly. On the contrary, progress in this direction is fraught with hazards and perils not less menacing than those born from want and suffering.

Many inventions are made with the goal of profit. The best inventions are ones that are intended to give happiness to the world, and my magnifying transmitter is one such invention. By its means, the human voice and likeness will be reproduced everywhere, and factories driven thousands of miles from waterfalls furnishing [their] power. Aerial machines will be propelled around the Earth without a stop, and the Sun's energy controlled to create lakes and rivers for motive purposes, and transformation of arid deserts into fertile

**land.** The magnifying transmitter will provide power for this and do so much more.

It will be hard to predict the quickly approaching trends if you simply read the newspapers. In matters of science, the press simply falls flat every time. The reporters learn to write very well, and they are educated, but many of them never learn to think critically concerning complicated subject matter. Let us take the problem of static interference, for example. One of our current problems with telecommunications is the static noise that may occur during a conversation over the telephone and radio.

Many men in the past ten years have claimed to have an idea that will fix the problem. None of them provided any solution in the end, but newspapers articles would have you believe the problem is as good as solved. A **recent official statement from the U.S. Navy** on the subject jumped to overly hopeful conclusions, and so now public opinion has shifted yet again. In my view, everything I've read in the newspapers about this kind of technology, even in the best papers, has been pure garbage.

Since the navy made its statement, more entrepreneurs have come forth to win the awe of the newspapers and to change their opinion yet again. One of our most reputable publications released an article with the **flourish of trumpets, but it proved [to be] another case of a mountain bringing forth a mouse.** The sensationalism in the news has corrupted journalistic integrity, but perhaps this is only human nature. In fact, **this reminds me of an exciting incident which took place years ago.**

That daredevil actor, Steve Brodie, **had just jumped off the Brooklyn Bridge.** Everyone was talking about it. Some other would-be daredevils gave an attempt in imitation, but with no result of causing the same uproar as Brodie. However, **the first report electrified New York.** I myself was caught up in the excitement, being of a more impressionable age than I am now.

**On a hot afternoon I felt the necessity of refreshing myself and stepped into one of the popular thirty thousand institutions of this great city, where a delicious twelve percent [alcoholic] beverage was served.** These days, the city is dry from the growing prohibition, but back then wines and spirits were plentiful. I was chatting with a fellow next to me at the bar and I made the joke towards the end of our conversation, **"This is what I said when I jumped off the bridge."**

I felt an immediate danger when I spoke these words. **In an instant, there was a pandemonium and a dozen voices cried, "It is Brodie!" I threw a quarter on the counter and bolted for the door, but the crowd was at my heels.** People yelled, **"Stop, Steve!"** For pedestrians on the street who did not know what was happening, many guessed that the crowd was chasing a thief, caught in the act, because the name Steve can sound an awful lot like the word "thief." Some began to echo, "Stop, thief!" Yet, they were just like the journalist, observing an incident and reporting a falsehood of what they witnessed.

Some people even tried to stop me, jutting in front of me or grabbing at my arm. I outran the crowd by taking advantage of the grid system of New York City, taking many turns to distance myself from the crowd. Then, I jumped up the fire escape into my laboratory, **where I threw off my coat, camouflaged myself as a hard-working blacksmith, and started the forge.** I pumped the bellows and hammered away at the anvil, but as I looked out the window, **these precautions proved unnecessary, as I had eluded my pursuers.**

It was a careless joke, and I have often wondered how badly the crowd could have ripped me into pieces had they discovered I was not Steve Brody. It is easy to make mistakes, such as my joke, but to say something incorrect in the newspapers is a much worse offense. There is a greater duty to be more careful with your words when they are put in print or said on a stage. The newspapers have done a very poor job of reporting on technology, though much of the issue may be more properly blamed on the general lack of scientific education as well as philosophy.

Recently, a renowned engineer **gave an account before a technical body of a novel remedy against [static interference] based on a "heretofore unknown law of nature."** The foundation for his argument rested on the fact that electrical disturbances in nature were entirely different from those observed between two ends of a man-made device. Essentially, he asserted that the Earth, acting as a capacitor, **with its gaseous envelope, could be charged and discharged in a manner quite contrary to the fundamental teachings propounded in every elemental text book of physics. Such a supposition would have been condemned as erroneous, even in Franklin's** time, for the facts bearing on this were then well known and the identity between atmospheric electricity and that developed by machines were common knowledge, even back then.

Obviously, natural and artificial disturbances propagate through the Earth and the air in exactly the same way, and both set up electromotive forces that extend out from both parallel and perpendicular to the axis of the disturbance. Interference cannot be overcome by any such methods as were proposed. The truth is this: In the air, the [electric] potential increases at the rate of about fifty volts per foot of elevation. Differences in air pressure can affect this number greatly and may create a difference of pressure amounting to twenty, or even forty thousand volts between the upper and lower ends of the antenna.

With this in mind, the masses of the charged atmosphere are constantly in motion and give up electricity to the conductor, not continuously, but rather disruptively, thus producing the crackly sound heard over the radio and telephone, commonly referred to as static noise. Static noise is wasted electrical energy that could be collected and used. The higher the terminal and the greater the space encompassed by the wires, the more pronounced is the effect, but it must be understood that it is purely local and has little to do with the real trouble.

In 1900, while perfecting my wireless system, I built a system composed of four antennae. **These were carefully calibrated to the same frequency** and connected in such a way that they essentially acted as directional receivers. In other words, if **I desired to ascertain the origin of the transmitted impulses**, I could simply compare the strength of the incoming signal for each tower. Some simple math would determine the answer to the distance and direction of the radio signal's origin. Additionally, static was reduced tremendously by grounding the employed receivers at two points in the ground. It was a simple and common sense change, but an instant improvement in the field of wireless receivers.

This was perfectly self-evident but came as a revelation to some simpleminded wireless folks whose experience was confined to forms of apparatus that could have been improved with an axe. But, as a matter of fact, a wire buried in the ground which, conforming to this view, should be absolutely immune, is

**more susceptible to certain extraneous impulses than one placed vertically in the air**.

In the short term, this will only be a small improvement for reducing static interference. I simply employed this method without much thought at all, taking only a small amount of time to improve the receivers I was using in my experiments. Although, **as I have said before, to dispose of this difficulty for good, a radical change must be made in the system and the sooner this is done the better.**

In a horrifying turn of recent events, a piece of legislation was proposed just a few weeks ago by Secretary Daniels. This measure would make the use and study of certain types of wireless transmission illegal for the commercial and private sectors. Only the government and the military will be allowed to use these technologies under the passing of this act. **Secretary Daniels has made his appeal to the Senate and House of Representatives with sincere conviction,** and it may have been convincing enough to sway both the House and the Senate. He fears that it would create catastrophic dangers to the public if everyone has access to radio communications.

The art of electricity is still new. The art of wireless electricity is even younger by comparison. Even the **experts have no conception of its ultimate possibilities.** For this and several other reasons, I very much disagree with Secretary Daniels' sentiments. The Great War was a calamity. I understand his fear that enemies would somehow take this technology to create a devastating weapon, but I see no reason to believe this. It is obvious to me that the benefits will outweigh the consequences, and I see little potential for negative effects at all.

In fact, there has never been an invention so beneficial to society as wireless transmission. It would be absurd to keep it away from the masses. History has shown us time and time again that competition creates the ideal situations for consumers, giving them more options at a cheaper price. A government monopoly will only slow the evolution of wireless technology. This paranoia is irrational and ill-founded.

Then again, it must be understood that this wonderful art has been, in its entirety, evolved here and can be called "American," with more right and propriety than the telephone, the incandescent lamp, or the airplane. Enterprising press agents and stock jobbers have been so successful in spreading misinformation, that even so excellent a periodical as the Scientific American accords the chief credit to a foreign country.

The Germans, of course gave us the Hertz waves and the Russians, English, French, and Italian experts were quick in using them for signaling purposes. Thus, the telegraph was born.

It was an obvious application of the new agent and accomplished with the old classical and unimproved induction coil, scarcely anything more than another kind of [trick using old methods]. The radius of transmission was very limited, the result attained of little value, and the Hertz oscillations, as a means of conveying intelligence, could have been advantageously replaced by sound waves, which I advocated in 1891. Moreover, all of these attempts were made three years after the basic principles of the wireless system, which is universally employed today, and its potent instrumentalities had been clearly described and developed in America.

No trace of those Hertzian appliances and methods remains today. We have proceeded in the very opposite direction and what has been done is the product of the brains and efforts of citizens of this country. The fundamental patents have expired, and the opportunities are open to all.

The chief argument of the Secretary is based on interference. According to his statement, reported in the New York Herald of July 29th [1919], signals from a powerful station can be intercepted in every village in the world. In view of this fact, which was demonstrated in my experiments in 1900, it would be of little use to impose restrictions in the United States.

Recently, a shady character approached me with an attempt of enlisting my services in the construction of world transmitters in some distant land. "We have no money," he said, "but carloads of solid gold, and we will give you a liberal amount." I told him that I wanted to see first what will be done with my inventions in America, and this ended the interview.

Passing a law to restrict the use of radio transmissions and other wireless communications may please the Democrats, but I am satisfied that some dark forces are at work [regardless of the law]. As time goes on, the maintenance of continuous communications will be rendered more difficult. The only remedy is a system immune against interruption.

**It has been perfected, it exists, and all that is necessary is to put it in operation.** My research in Colorado and my tower at Long Island was the first step towards this great future of many possibilities.

This colossal war has just ended, and threat of violence still hangs in the air. The fear of this technology is nonsense, because it would only improve our national defense. This is most true **particularly in connection with telautomatics.** Just like the remote controlled toy submarine[10] I created, a full-scale warship could be controlled at a remote distance.

For a while, **I really thought that [this invention of mine] would abolish war, because of its unlimited destructiveness** and for the ability it will create in replacing human foot soldiers with machines. Although, I still see much promise in this invention for its potential to improve the world, **my views have changed since.** Technology alone will not end war.

The social conditions that cause war must be solved before any threat of violence is to be

---

[10] Although his first product was a working remote-controlled boat, Tesla tells us that he soon made improvements to the device. This included submersible properties.

nullified. When there are enough resources to share among all nations, it will drastically reduce any threat of war. Electric energy has become a resource like any other, and the ability to distribute large amounts of it to all people will likely be a large step towards world peace.

The true problem of war and violence is that it is the nature of man. **All over the Earth, [we must strive for] the elimination of that fanatic devotion to exalted ideals of national egoism and pride.** Superstition and bigotry are the birth parents of large-scale human violence. No vote, no politician, no union, no law, and no social movement of any kind will ever pacify the brutal nature of the world.

**Peace can only come as a natural consequence of universal enlightenment and merging of races, and we are still far from this blissful realization.** Religious zealotry is one primary cause of war, but it will be many years before the followers of Christ, Muhammad, and the Jewish peoples can accept that they worship the same God of Abraham. The Eastern story of Krishna is alike to the story of Christ. We are all one people, and we serve the same God.

**As I view the world of today, in the light of the gigantic struggle we have witnessed, I am**

filled with the conviction that the interest of humanity would be best served if the United States remained true to its traditions, true to God, and kept out of entangling alliances [as the founding fathers warned]. Situated as it is, geographically remote from the theaters of impending conflicts, without incentive to territorial aggrandizement, with inexhaustible resources and immense population thoroughly imbued with the spirit of liberty and [justice], this country is placed in a unique and privileged position. It is thus able to exert, independently, its colossal strength and moral force to the benefit of all, more judiciously and effectively, than as a member of a league.

I have told you about my strange medical condition of hallucinations that has affected me since my childhood. This strange ailment was **at first involuntary, [and] gradually became second nature and led me finally to recognize that I was but an automation devoid of free will in thought and action and merely responsible to the forces of the [immediate surrounding] environment.**

We are a creature that has evolved slowly for countless generations. Charles Darwin's observations are succinct in showing us this. Our senses are delicately calibrated to be very strong, but we are so complicated that most people have lost connection to the avatar of their body. They live only within the realm of lofty ideas, impractical and romantic wishful thinking that bears little resemblance to reality. **It is hard for the average person to grasp this fact**.

As a scientist, and a seeker of truth, I am convinced of the philosophy of mechanism, which was **propounded by Descartes three hundred years ago.** Although men in Descartes' time did not have a strong understanding of biology, his ideas still remain true. Now, we have a much better understanding of the **construction and operation of the eye**, for example. Yet, I see the reflection of Descartes' rationalist approach in Darwin's theory. Each generation of thinkers has further advanced our connection to the truth, one step at a time.

**In recent years, the scientific research in these fields has been such as to leave no room for a doubt [as to whether or not they are true].** Felix le Dantec, for example, has performed some of my favorite work in biology for his experiments in showing the directional growth of plant-life in response to sunlight.[11] Everything seems to become one with the surroundings.

Although educated people understand all of these ideas to be truth, the average person still does not. I see these realities clearly with **every act and thought of mine.** A firm concentration on the many influences that affect my mood and decision making is **ever present in my mind.** I can generally account for any of my thoughts by **locating the original impulse** in the body that created them. **The by far greater number of human beings are never aware of** their own highly impressionable nature, nor can they feel their own body with an acute awareness.

Because of this, millions of people have developed bad habits that make them sick or give them chronic pain, even leading them to an early death when they could have lived a long, healthy life. They have no concept for how the world around them continually functions to affect them. For these unfortunate people, they are completely lost for knowledge on how to maintain their own health. **The commonest, everyday**

---

[11] Tesla also recommends Jacques Loeb's book on the subject, *Forced Movements*.

occurrences appear to them mysterious and inexplicable. One may feel a sudden wave of sadness and rack his brain for an explanation, when he might have noticed that it was caused by a cloud cutting off the rays of the sun.

Deficient observation is merely a form of ignorance, [one of many which is] responsible for the many morbid notions and foolish ideas prevailing. Idiocy and willful ignorance are rampant in our society. In fact, I would propose that there is not more than one out of every ten persons who does not believe in telepathy or some other psychic manifestations, spiritualism, or other beliefs whereby it would seem that an otherwise rational person proves to be completely unreasonable. What's worse, the majority of people seem to be captivated by talk of the supernatural and other utter poppycock.

Just to illustrate how deeply rooted this tendency has become even among the clear-headed American population, I may mention a comical incident. Before the war broke out, when people were still interested in commercial innovation, there was a small buzz about my new bladeless turbines after I exhibited them in New York City. I anticipated that there

**would be a scramble among manufacturers to get hold of the invention, and I had particular designs** drafted specifically for Mister Henry Ford, in the event I could interest him.

I was sure that people from his organization would inevitably come knocking on my door. I told everyone that worked in my front office to expect a visit from a Ford representative. **Sure enough, one fine morning a body of engineers from the Ford Motor Company presented themselves with the request of discussing with me an important project.**

My secretary led them into a boardroom, and I began to give a speech about my turbines. One of the men **interrupted me and said, "We know all about this, but we are on a special errand. We have formed a psychological society for the investigation of psychic phenomena and we want you to join us in the undertaking."** I walked straight out of the room. I wanted to shout at these imbeciles for succumbing to such stupidity. **These engineers never knew how near they came to being fired out of my office.**

Belief in the supernatural is nothing but childishness. I have only one time encountered anything that I considered might be supernatural. I was fooled by my emotions, and

I was still at the time dumbstruck by the death of my mother. The emotional pain of losing her had rendered me unable to think properly, and feelings of loneliness possessed me.

I was spending some time in London with my friend, Sir William Crookes. When I was in college, I read Crookes's writings on electricity and the atomic structure. His ideas captivated me and furthered my obsession with the mysterious thing called electricity. I would have never let another person convince me of nonsense, but I very much respected Sir Crookes, and so I listened to him with an open mind.

When my mother was dying, I became as gullible as he. Years after meeting with Sir Crookes, as I was frantically returning to my boyhood home to see my mother, I soon collapsed after reaching town. Some townsfolk carried me into their home to help me recover. Once I regained partial consciousness, I realized I was staying **about two blocks from our home.** However, I did not have the strength to stand upright.

That night, as I was alone in a stranger's house, I worried desperately about my mother's life. I would soon reunite with my family to discover that she had indeed already passed, but at the time I was clueless. In my debilitated state, I called on my mother from beyond the void to show me a sign if she had indeed left this world. I begged her not to leave without telling me goodbye.

I stayed awake until the early morning, straining my eyes for some magical sign. I was still awake at sunrise, and when I finally fell to sleep, I dreamed of my mother. In my dream, I was in the very same room, still waiting for her to give me a sign and speak to me. A cloud of smoke and light suddenly appeared in the room. **Angelic figures of marvelous beauty** floated at a distance above my bed, **one of whom gazed upon me lovingly and gradually assumed the features of my mother.**

She spoke to me briefly, and then left. Her and the other angels floated out of the window, and I woke up. **I was awakened by an indescribably sweet song of many voices.** When I heard the music as I woke up, I was sure it was coming from another world, somehow. The truth is that I was bewildered, and a nearby Sunday choir was performing their hymns for worship. I was certain that my mother had contacted me from beyond the grave.

I was fooled from these visions for a short time, and in my estranged state of mind, I thought I had actually witnessed the spirit of my mother. When I regained my bodily functions, I walked over to my old home to meet again with my family. The news of her death only served to reinforce my belief that her ghostly appearance had visited me the previous night.

I was sure of this for several weeks, still processing the trauma of her death. When I finally recovered my senses, I pondered on this occurrence. To begin with, the vision merely appeared in a dream. There is nothing so spectacular about that, but it seemed so real that I did not know it to be a dream. Furthermore, if my waking mind was so fixated on thoughts of seeing my mother, it would be no surprise to think that perhaps my sleeping mind maintained that same intense focus of thought on a single subject.

The music from the nearby church made my mind think about angels. I even remembered the formation of the angels appearing in my dream, and realized that they appeared in the same shape of a famous painting of angels I had seen many times. The mind is so extremely susceptible to self-trickery from an abundance of outside influences.

Very often, people have emotional moments and point to the supernatural as an explanation for life and purpose. I dare say that anyone who claims to have seen evidence of actual supernatural experiences was certainly in some state of excitement that clouded their judgement, letting their enthusiasm get the best of them. I put the respected scientist, Sir William Crookes, in this category just as well.[12]

**There is absolutely no foundation** of facts proven by the critical methods of science for anything related to **psychical and spiritual phenomena.** These are senseless beliefs of superstition, but I understand why it is so captivating for people to believe in them. The people of the world are growing more intellectual, and the orthodox views of God are becoming more relaxed. People are enlightened enough to know that many of the old ways of thinking about religion are obviously inconsistent with reality. The way of faith, like all things, is bound to evolve.

---

[12] Sir William Crookes was a renowned scientist, the inventor of the radiometer, and the discoverer of the element Thallium. Late in his career, he became a serious believer in ghosts.

Yet, as people outgrow the old and ignorant forms of the faith, **every individual clings to [the belief of] a supreme power of some kind.** As people stray from the teaching of the Scriptures, unable to reconcile modern and factual knowledge with the wonderful stories of creation, they embrace any new message of spiritual harmony that presents itself to them. It may lead them to believing in ghosts, or believing that the planet Mercury has a greater effect on their life than their immediate surroundings. People are hungry for God when they lose their faith, almost like a void that must be filled in the creation of a vacuum.

People need structure in their lives to **insure contentment.** It does not matter **whether it be one of [religion], art, science, or anything else, so long as it fulfills the function of a [productive] force.** But if we are to talk of God, **it is essential to the peaceful existence of humanity as a whole that one common conception should prevail.** In turn, we need science to give us a uniform idea of where we come from, and for the discoveries of undeniable truths. No argument of one prophet over another will ever prevail to make converts of faithful men, but science can unify all religions.

In addition to the biologist I have previously mentioned, and the proven theory of evolution by natural selection, I have satisfied myself in developing my own theory of **the automatism of life.** I have been developing these observations since my boyhood, and everything I continue to see suggests to confirm them.

**I got the first inkling of this astonishing truth when I was still a very young man. For many years I interpreted what I noted simply as coincidences**, but then I returned to them with a serious level of scrutiny. In private, I have swayed the opinion of many friends on this subject, **which may be stated in the following few words: our bodies are of similar construction and exposed to the same external forces.** Everything in the universe is constantly changing in relation to its surroundings.

We are no different, and it is my view that as a species, **we are automata entirely controlled by the forces of the medium, being tossed about like corks on the surface of the water but mistaking the resultant of the impulses from the outside for the free will.** We make all of our decisions, social or otherwise, based on a deeply ingrained instinct for survival. We cannot control our emotions, but we can reflect on them and understand the obviousness as to why they arose. It seems to me, our neural wiring is programmed with many sensitive triggers to a barrage of emotional action, whether it be excitement or fear, or some other heightened emotion. It is simply stimulus and stimulant, and every thought and desire can be traced back to the survival instinct.

**Everybody understands, of course, that if one becomes deaf, has his eyes weakened, or his limbs injured, his [quality of life is] lessened. But this is also true, and perhaps more so, of certain defects in the brain which deprive the automaton, more or less, of that vital quality and cause it to rush into destruction.**

If we are an automaton, I thought, perhaps we can build mechanical automatons. I first set out to build a machine in 1895, **when I started my wireless investigations. During the [following] two or three years, a number of automatic mechanisms, to be [controlled] from a distance, were constructed by me and exhibited to visitors in my laboratory.**

I designed a small robot in 1896 and built the first model in 1897. The following year, I was granted a patent for my draft of the invention, **but only after the examiner-in-chief had come to New York to witness the performance** of this machine for himself. **It created a sensation such as no other invention of mine has ever produced.** People simply could not believe their eyes.

The machine could do a few common chores and tasks with the press of a button. **I remember that when later I called on an official in Washington, with a view of offering the invention to the government, he burst out in laughter upon my telling him what I had accomplished. Nobody thought then that there was the faintest prospect of perfecting such a device**.

I will happily divulge a secret to you now. **Following the advice of my attorneys,** the drawing for my patent on this robot indicated that the power source was controlled by a single circuit. I have developed many ways whereby power can be distributed more efficiently by looping a series of circuits together. I had not yet been granted patents for these methods, and so to protect them, I was advised to employ secrecy. In the patent drawings, I used the same circuit boards that were commonplace at the time.

In demonstrating my [robot] before audiences, the visitors were requested to ask questions, however involved, and the automaton would answer them by signs. **This was considered magic at the time, but was extremely simple, for it was me who gave the replies by means of the device.** With a remote, I could tap Morse code, and the lights installed on the robot submarine would answer any questions asked by the audience.

This was only my second version of the device. I had made some slight improvements from the first. **For example, incandescent lamps** were placed throughout the device to show **visible evidence of the proper functioning of the machine.** I also improved the strength of the watertight seal. The lights also made it easier for the user to see and control the machine. **[These] were the first and rather crude steps [toward] the evolution of the art of telautomatics**, and people will continue to perfect this idea for centuries to come.

After I made these machines, **the next logical improvement was its application to automatic mechanisms beyond the limits of vision and at great distances from the center of control.** In other words, the machines need to be able to do more work with less human supervision. A day will come when this will be a reality. It will lead to the largest advancement of society ever recorded.

**I have devoted years of study to this matter and have evolved means, making [these] wonders easily realizable.** People will continue to find completely new uses for these ideas for generations to come, and gradually all human work will be replaced by the work of machines.

Even the dirty work of war will be done by machines. The flying machine I intended to create while studying in college is an idea I occasionally returned to in my adulthood. **I conceived a flying machine quite unlike the present ones**[13]. One day, machines like these will be able to fly without a person controlling from the cockpit. I have also drafted a separate invention for **aerial machines sustained and propelled entirely by reaction.**

These machines will have many possible ways of control, and they will be precise in their use for warfare. **By installing proper plants, it will be [possible] to project a missile of this kind into the air and drop it** on

---

[13] Drawings Tesla made of his "flying machine" much more resemble a crude helicopter than an airplane.

practically any spot on the globe. Even at a distance of **thousands of miles away.**[14]

Innovation in the field will **not stop at this. Telautomats will be ultimately produced, capable of acting as if possessed of their own intelligence, and their advent will create a revolution.** In 1898, I met with the appropriate company board members to pitch them the idea to use my inventions to create an automobile that can drive itself. They thought the idea was poorly described and did not believe for a moment that such a thing could be possible.

This Great War has only just ended, and right now **many of the ablest minds are trying to devise [ways of] preventing a repetition of the awful conflict, which [has] only theoretically ended. The proposed [League of Nations] is not a remedy, but on the contrary, in the opinion of a number of competent men [and myself], may bring about results just the opposite.**

Punishing Germany so harshly by the treaty will create suffering for the German

---

[14] This was 1919 and the first missile of this description was used during World War II in 1944, one year after Tesla's death. The weapon was used by Nazi Germany and created by Dr. Wernher Von Braun.

people for years to come. Conditions will be prime for the reignition of war in Europe. There will be much poverty and resentment as a result of the allied attempts at restorative justice. This eye for an eye mentality will ensure that the war does not come to an end, and violence will erupt again in Europe.

**It is particularly regrettable that [this] policy [to so harshly punish the losers of the war] was adopted [for] the terms of peace.** In a matter of years, not decades, **it will be possible for nations to fight without armies, ships, or guns, by weapons far more terrible. The destructive [power] of [modern militaries will soon] virtually [have] no limit.**

By taking away Germany's air force and navy, and making their government pay the devastating cost for French reparations, there will remain heavy tensions in Europe. The next war may see some of the most gruesome tactics the world has ever seen. In the very near future, **any city, at a distance whatsoever from the enemy, can be destroyed** on demand. There will be **no power on Earth [that] can stop [nations] from doing so**. Once the buttons are pressed, the weapons will unleash their doom.

If we are to create peace, one thing must be done **without an instant's delay, and with all the power and resources of the nation.** We must distribute abundant amounts of electricity to all people around the globe. For the purpose of world peace, I have developed ample methods of executing this great act.

I am long past my prime, but all that is left is for future generations to pick up where I left off. **If we want to avert an impending calamity and a state of things which may transform this globe into an inferno, we should push the development of wireless transmission of energy.** Alleviating human struggle and poverty will be one of the most effective ways for creating a world without large-scale violence.

# A Note on Quotations

Several of the quotes inserted throughout this book have been modified to conform to 21st century grammar, or to fit the surrounding text and context. For example, Tesla would often capitalize nouns that were not proper nouns, such as "Public Library," and "City Park." Commas have also been modified in some quotes to make the sentence more clear.

While no quotes have been falsified or augmented, a select few quotes were shortened to increase clarity by omitting words or phrases. Furthermore, many of Tesla's quotes vary slightly from one printed copy of his autobiography to another. The most extreme cases of using modified quotes are listed below with page numbers for reference. All of these quotes can be found in *The Autobiography of Nikola Tesla*, also known as *My Inventions*.

Pg. 32: "There is scarcely a subject that cannot be mathematically treated and the effects calculated or the results determined beforehand from the available theoretical and practical data." (The middle of this quote was cut for brevity.)

Pg. 45: "Friends of mine often remark that my suits fit me like gloves but they do not know that all my clothing is made to measurements which were taken nearly fifteen years ago and never changed." (The verb tense of "is made" was changed to "was made.")

Pg. 46: "He was employed for a long time in a Chicago slaughter-house where he weighed thousands of hogs every day! That's why." (Exclamation omitted in this book.)

Pg. 75: "We are whirling through endless space with an inconceivable speed, all around us everything is spinning, everything is moving, everywhere is energy." (The original was a run-on sentence, and was made into two sentences.)

Pg. 108: Some versions of Tesla's writing say, "Bachelor, this is a *damn* good man,"

Note: Some sources spell his name "Charles Bachelor" and some spell it "Batchelor" or Batchellor."

Pg. 132: Some versions of Tesla's autobiography say: "I will be quite explicit on the subject of my magnifying transformer so that it will be clearly understood."

This is the original text: "I have been asked by the ELECTRICAL EXPERIMENTER to be quite explicit on this subject so that my young friends among the readers of the magazine will clearly understand the construction and operation of my "magnifying transmitter" and the purposes for which it is intended."

Pg. 133: "Theoretically, a terminal of less than 90 feet in diameter is sufficient to develop an electromotive force of that magnitude while for antenna currents of from 2,000-4,000 amperes at the usual frequencies it need not be larger than 30 feet in diameter." (This quote was shortened for brevity.)

Pg. 133: "Such a circuit may then be excited with impulses of any kind, even of low frequency and it will yield sinusoidal and continuous oscillations like those of an alternator." (The word sinusoidal was omitted for brevity and clarity.)

Pg. 161: In some versions it is printed: "as I have said before," but it appears the original text is: "As I pointed out in a previous article."

Pg. 161: "This was proposed a few weeks ago by Secretary Daniels, and no doubt that distinguished official has made his appeal to the Senate and House of Representatives with sincere conviction." This quote was shortened to: "Secretary Daniels has made his appeal to the Senate and House of Representatives with sincere conviction."

Pg. 162: "It would be calamitous, indeed, if at this time when the art is in its infancy and the vast majority, not excepting even experts, have no conception of its ultimate possibilities, a measure would be rushed through the legislature making it a government monopoly." This quote was shortened to read: "Experts have no conception of its ultimate possibilities."

Pg. 167: In many versions, the following phrase is omitted completely: "...If the United States remained true to its traditions, true to God, whom it pretends to believe..."

Pg. 167: "This mental activity, at first involuntary under the pressure of illness and suffering, gradually became second nature and led me finally to recognize that I was but an automaton devoid of free will in thought and action and merely responsive to the forces of the environment." The words "under pressure of illness" were omitted for brevity.

Pg. 184: The words "flying machines and" where omitted from the final quote in the book: "We should push the development of flying machines and wireless transmission of energy."

"Art is a lie that makes us realize truth."
—Pablo Picasso

# Further Reading

I. Nikola Tesla's *Colorado Spring Notes*
of 1899-1900
(For those who can read physics equations)

II. *Nikola Tesla: Man of the Future*
An interview by Curtis Brown

III. *My Inventions*:
The Autobiography of Nikola Tesla

IV. *The Problem of Increasing Human Energy*
by Nikola Tesla

V. *The True Wireless* by Nikola Tesla

VI. *Wizard: The Life and Times of Nikola Tesla:
Biography of a Genius*
by Marc Seifer

# About the Author

Ellis Oswalt is a writer, producer, and classically trained actor who lives in New York City. Find out more at Ellisoswalt.com